THE POCKET TREASURY OF BIBLE PROMISES

THE POCKET TREASURY OF BIBLE PROMISES

Featuring Selections from The King James Version of the Bible

FRONTPORCH
BOOKS

The Pocket Treasury of Bible Promises

Published by Garborgs
P.O. Box 20132, Bloomington, MN 55420
To order call 800/678-5727

ISBN 1-58375-476-8

Produced for Garborgs by The Livingstone Corporation.
Project Staff include: Christopher D. Hudson, Paige Haley,
Amber Rae, Lindsay Vanker.

Printed and bound in the United States of America.

The Word of God is a living treasure, more valuable than jewels or riches. The Bible contains the answers to every question of life, and each time you read and meditate on Scripture, the Lord feeds and nourishes your spirit. This treasury highlights promises that will encourage you daily. As you read them, adopt each verse as your own; the Bible is God's way of speaking to you.

TABLE OF CONTENTS

ACCEPTANCE

Does God accept me as the person I am?

Deuteronomy 7:6

For thou art an holy people unto the Lord thy God: the Lord thy God hath chosen thee to be a special people unto himself, above all people that are upon the face of the earth.

Psalm 100:3

Know ye that the Lord he is God: it is he that hath made us, and not we ourselves; we are his people, and the sheep of his pasture.

John 6:37

All that the Father giveth me shall come to me; and him that cometh to me I will in no wise cast out.

Ephesians 2:10

For we are his workmanship, created in Christ Jesus unto good works, which God hath before ordained that we should walk in them.

To whom do I belong?

Isaiah 43:1

But now thus saith the LORD that created thee, O Jacob, and he that formed thee, O Israel, Fear not: for I have redeemed thee, I have called *thee* by thy name; thou *art* mine.

Romans 14:8

For whether we live, we live unto the Lord; and whether we die, we die unto the Lord: whether we live therefore, or die, we are the Lord's.

Jeremiah 31:3

The LORD hath appeared of old unto me, *saying,* Yea, I have loved thee with an everlasting love: therefore with lovingkindness have I drawn thee.

Isaiah 49:15-16

Can a woman forget her sucking child, that she should not have compassion on the son of her womb? yea, they may forget, yet will I not forget thee. Behold, I have graven thee upon the palms of *my* hands; thy walls *are* continually before me.

How should I accept others?

Romans 15:7
Wherefore receive ye one another, as Christ also received us to the glory of God.

Romans 14:1
Him that is weak in the faith receive ye, *but* not to doubtful disputations.

Matthew 7:2
For with what judgment ye judge, ye shall be judged: and with what measure ye mete, it shall be measured to you again.

James 2:2-4
For if there come unto your assembly a man with a gold ring, in goodly apparel, and there come in also a poor man in vile raiment; And ye have respect to him that weareth the gay clothing, and say unto him, Sit thou here in a good place; and say to the poor, Stand thou there, or sit here under my footstool: Are ye not then partial in yourselves, and are become judges of evil thoughts?

BLESSING

On whom will God shower blessings?

Psalm 1:1-2

Blessed *is* the man that walketh not in the counsel of the ungodly, nor standeth in the way of sinners, nor sitteth in the seat of the scornful. But his delight *is* in the law of the LORD; and in his law doth he meditate day and night.

Deuteronomy 11:26-27

Behold, I set before you this day a blessing and a curse; A blessing, if ye obey the commandments of the LORD your God, which I command you this day.

James 4:6

But he giveth more grace. Wherefore he saith, God resisteth the proud, but giveth grace unto the humble.

Isaiah 44:3

For I will pour water upon him that is thirsty, and floods upon the dry ground: I will pour my spirit upon thy seed, and my blessing upon thine offspring.

Jeremiah 17:7

Blessed *is* the man that trusteth in the LORD, and whose hope the LORD is.

What does God give as his blessings?

James 1:17

Every good gift and every perfect gift is from above, and cometh down from the Father of lights, with whom is no variableness, neither shadow of turning.

Malachi 3:10

Bring ye all the tithes into the storehouse, that there may be meat in mine house, and prove me now herewith, saith the LORD of hosts, if I will not open you the windows of heaven, and pour you out a blessing, that *there shall* not *be room* enough *to receive it.*

Psalm 103:2-3

Bless the LORD, O my soul, and forget not all his benefits: Who forgiveth all thine iniquities; who healeth all thy diseases.

Ezekiel 34:26-27

And I will make them and the places round about my hill a blessing; and I will cause the shower to come down in his season; there shall be showers of blessing. And the tree of the field shall yield her fruit, and the earth shall yield her increase, and they shall be safe in their land, and shall know that I *am* the LORD, when I have broken the bands of their yoke, and delivered them out of the hand of those that served themselves of them.

Am I to bless others?

Numbers 6:24-26
The LORD bless thee, and keep thee: The LORD make his face shine upon thee, and be gracious unto thee: The LORD lift up his countenance upon thee, and give thee peace.

Romans 12:14
Bless them which persecute you: bless, and curse not.

1 Peter 3:9
Not rendering evil for evil, or railing for railing: but contrariwise blessing; knowing that ye are thereunto called, that ye should inherit a blessing.

COMFORT

Who will be my comfort?

Isaiah 66:13

As one whom his mother comforteth, so will I comfort you; and ye shall be comforted in Jerusalem.

Psalm 23:4

Yea, though I walk through the valley of the shadow of death, I will fear no evil: for thou *art* with me; thy rod and thy staff they comfort me.

Revelation 7:17

For the Lamb which is in the midst of the throne shall feed them, and shall lead them unto living fountains of waters: and God shall wipe away all tears from their eyes.

Matthew 11:28-30

Come unto me, all *ye* that labour and are heavy laden, and I will give you rest. Take my yoke upon you, and learn of me; for I am meek and lowly in heart: and ye shall find rest unto your souls. For my yoke *is* easy, and my burden is light.

How can I comfort others?

2 Corinthians 1:3-4

Blessed *be* God, even the Father of our Lord Jesus Christ, the Father of mercies, and the God of all comfort; Who comforteth us in all our tribulation, that we may be able to comfort them which are in any trouble, by the comfort wherewith we ourselves are comforted of God.

Romans 12:15

Rejoice with them that do rejoice, and weep with them that weep.

Isaiah 40:1

Comfort ye, comfort ye my people, saith your God.

Galatians 6:2

Bear ye one another's burdens, and so fulfil the law of Christ.

COMPASSION

How great is God's compassion?

Psalm 119:156

Great *are* thy tender mercies, O LORD: quicken me according to thy judgments.

Lamentations 3:22-23

It is of the LORD's mercies that we are not consumed, because his compassions fail not. *They are* new every morning: great *is* thy faithfulness.

Nehemiah 9:17

But thou *art* a God ready to pardon, gracious and merciful, slow to anger, and of great kindness, and forsookest them not.

Isaiah 54:10

For the mountains shall depart, and the hills be removed; but my kindness shall not depart from thee, neither shall the covenant of my peace be removed, saith the LORD that hath mercy on thee.

Will God show compassion to me?

Hosea 2:19

And I will betroth thee unto me for ever; yea, I will betroth thee unto me in righteousness, and in judgment, and in lovingkindness, and in mercies.

Psalm 103:13

Like as a father pitieth *his* children, *so* the LORD pitieth them that fear him.

Psalm 145:9

The LORD *is* good to all: and his tender mercies *are* over all his works.

Isaiah 30:18

And therefore will the LORD wait, that he may be gracious unto you, and therefore will he be exalted, that he may have mercy upon you: for the LORD *is* a God of judgment: blessed *are* all they that wait for him.

CONFIDENCE

Can I place my confidence fully in God?

Romans 8:38-39

For I am persuaded, that neither death, nor life, nor angels, nor principalities, nor powers, nor things present, nor things to come, Nor height, nor depth, nor any other creature, shall be able to separate us from the love of God, which is in Christ Jesus our Lord.

Isaiah 54:10

For the mountains shall depart, and the hills be removed; but my kindness shall not depart from thee, neither shall the covenant of my peace be removed, saith the LORD that hath mercy on thee.

Job 41:11

Who hath prevented me, that I should repay *him?* *whatsoever is* under the whole heaven is mine.

Isaiah 26:4

Trust ye in the LORD for ever: for in the LORD JEHOVAH *is* everlasting strength.

Psalm 118:8

It is better to trust in the LORD than to put confidence in man.

Should I live with confidence?

Hebrews 13:6

So that we may boldly say, The Lord *is* my helper, and I will not fear what man shall do unto me.

Psalm 27:1

The LORD *is* my light and my salvation; whom shall I fear? the LORD *is* the strength of my life; of whom shall I be afraid?

Isaiah 32:17

And the work of righteousness shall be peace; and the effect of righteousness quietness and assurance for ever.

1 John 5:14-15

And this is the confidence that we have in him, that, if we ask any thing according to his will, he heareth us: And if we know that he hear us, whatsoever we ask, we know that we have the petitions that we desired of him.

Hebrews 11:1

Now faith is the substance of things hoped for, the evidence of things not seen.

Can I approach hard times with confidence?

Psalm 23:4
Yea, though I walk through the valley of the shadow of death, I will fear no evil: for thou *art* with me; thy rod and thy staff they comfort me.

Psalm 27:3
Though an host should encamp against me, my heart shall not fear: though war should rise against me, in this *will* I *be* confident.

Hebrews 4:16
Let us therefore come boldly unto the throne of grace, that we may obtain mercy, and find grace to help in time of need.

Matthew 11:28
Come unto me, all ye that labour and are heavy laden, and I will give you rest.

Can I be confident of my eternal salvation?

2 Timothy 1:12

For the which cause I also suffer these things: nevertheless I am not ashamed: for I know whom I have believed, and am persuaded that he is able to keep that which I have committed unto him against that day.

1 John 2:28

And now, little children, abide in him; that, when he shall appear, we may have confidence, and not be ashamed before him at his coming.

John 10:27-29

My sheep hear my voice, and I know them, and they follow me: And I give unto them eternal life; and they shall never perish, neither shall any *man* pluck them out of my hand. My Father, which gave *them* me, is greater than all; and no *man* is able to pluck *them* out of my Father's hand.

Psalm 62:1-2

Truly my soul waiteth upon God: from him *cometh* my salvation. He only *is* my rock and my salvation; *he is* my defence; I shall not be greatly moved.

Job 19:25

For I know that my redeemer liveth, and that he shall stand at the latter day upon the earth.

CONTENTMENT

Does my spirit find contentment in God?

Psalm 16:2
O my soul, thou hast said unto the LORD, Thou *art* my Lord: my goodness *extendeth* not to thee.

Psalm 37:4
Delight thyself also in the LORD; and he shall give thee the desires of thine heart.

Psalm 46:10
Be still, and know that I *am* God: I will be exalted among the heathen, I will be exalted in the earth.

Philippians 4:6-7
Be careful for nothing; but in every thing by prayer and supplication with thanksgiving let your requests be made known unto God. And the peace of God, which passeth all understanding, shall keep your hearts and minds through Christ Jesus.

2 Peter 1:3
According as his divine power hath given unto us all things that *pertain* unto life and godliness, through the knowledge of him that hath called us to glory and virtue.

Can I be content in wealth or in poverty?

Philippians 4:11-12

Not that I speak in respect of want: for I have learned, in whatsoever state I am, *therewith* to be content. I know both how to be abased, and I know how to abound: every where and in all things I am instructed both to be full and to be hungry, both to abound and to suffer need.

1 Timothy 6:6-7

But godliness with contentment is great gain. For we brought nothing into *this* world, *and it is* certain we can carry nothing out.

Hebrews 13:5

Let your conversation *be* without covetousness; *and be* content with such things as ye have: for he hath said, I will never leave thee, nor forsake thee.

Ecclesiastes 2:24

There is nothing better for a man, *than* that he should eat and drink, and *that* he should make his soul enjoy good in his labour. This also I saw, that it *was* from the hand of God.

1 Timothy 6:8

And having food and raiment let us be therewith content.

Can God help me to be content even in times of pain?

Job 1:21
And said, Naked came I out of my mother's womb, and naked shall I return thither: the LORD gave, and the LORD hath taken away; blessed be the name of the LORD.

Luke 6:21
Blessed *are ye* that hunger now: for ye shall be filled. Blessed *are ye* that weep now: for ye shall laugh.

Psalm 23:1-2
The LORD *is* my shepherd; I shall not want. He maketh me to lie down in green pastures: he leadeth me beside the still waters.

Psalm 27:13-14
I had fainted, unless I had believed to see the goodness of the LORD in the land of the living. Wait on the LORD: be of good courage, and he shall strengthen thine heart: wait, I say, on the LORD.

COURAGE

Does God want me to be courageous?

Joshua 1:9

Have not I commanded thee? Be strong and of a good courage; be not afraid, neither be thou dismayed: for the LORD thy God *is* with thee whithersoever thou goest.

Isaiah 41:10

Fear thou not; for I *am* with thee: be not dismayed; for I *am* thy God: I will strengthen thee; yea, I will help thee; yea, I will uphold thee with the right hand of my righteousness.

Isaiah 43:2-3

When thou passest through the waters, I *will be* with thee; and through the rivers, they shall not overflow thee: when thou walkest through the fire, thou shalt not be burned; neither shall the flame kindle upon thee. For I *am* the LORD thy God, the Holy One of Israel, thy Saviour: I gave Egypt *for* thy ransom, Ethiopia and Seba for thee.

What is the source of my courage?

Deuteronomy 7:21

Thou shalt not be affrighted at them: for the LORD thy God *is* among you, a mighty God and terrible.

Psalm 18:32-33

It is God that girdeth me with strength, and maketh my way perfect. He maketh my feet like hinds' *feet,* and setteth me upon my high places.

Psalm 18:29

For by thee I have run through a troop; and by my God have I leaped over a wall.

Isaiah 50:7

For the Lord GOD will help me; therefore shall I not be confounded: therefore have I set my face like a flint, and I know that I shall not be ashamed.

Does courage ever require patience, not action?

Psalm 27:14
Wait on the LORD: be of good courage, and he shall strengthen thine heart: wait, I say, on the LORD.

Psalm 31:24
Be of good courage, and he shall strengthen your heart, all ye that hope in the LORD.

Isaiah 40:29
He giveth power to the faint; and to *them that have* no might he increaseth strength.

Isaiah 40:31
But they that wait upon the LORD shall renew *their* strength; they shall mount up with wings as eagles; they shall run, and not be weary; *and* they shall walk, and not faint.

Exodus 14:14
The LORD shall fight for you, and ye shall hold your peace.

DELIVERANCE

From whom will my deliverance come?

2 Samuel 22:2

And he said, The LORD *is* my rock, and my fortress, and my deliverer.

Psalm 34:7

The angel of the LORD encampeth round about them that fear him, and delivereth them.

Psalm 91:14-15

Because he hath set his love upon me, therefore will I deliver him: I will set him on high, because he hath known my name. He shall call upon me, and I will answer him: I *will be* with him in trouble; I will deliver him, and honour him.

Deuteronomy 32:39

See now that I, *even* I, *am* he, and *there is* no god with me: I kill, and I make alive; I wound, and I heal: neither *is there any* that can deliver out of my hand.

Job 19:25

For I know *that* my redeemer liveth, and *that* he shall stand at the latter *day* upon the earth.

Can I hope for deliverance from my trials?

Psalm 34:17
The righteous cry, and the LORD heareth, and delivereth them out of all their troubles.

Psalm 107:6
Then they cried unto the LORD in their trouble, *and* he delivered them out of their distresses.

2 Peter 2:9
The Lord knoweth how to deliver the godly out of temptations, and to reserve the unjust unto the day of judgment to be punished.

Psalm 32:7
Thou *art* my hiding place; thou shalt preserve me from trouble; thou shalt compass me about with songs of deliverance. Selah.

Psalm 116:8
For thou hast delivered my soul from death, mine eyes from tears, *and* my feet from falling.

DISCERNMENT

How can I discern the truth?

John 14:16
And I will pray the Father, and he shall give you another Comforter, that he may abide with you for ever.

John 14:26
But the Comforter, *which is* the Holy Ghost, whom the Father will send in my name, he shall teach you all things, and bring all things to your remembrance, whatsoever I have said unto you.

John 16:13
Howbeit when he, the Spirit of truth, is come, he will guide you into all truth: for he shall not speak of himself; but whatsoever he shall hear, *that* shall he speak: and he will shew you things to come.

John 16:15
All things that the Father hath are mine: therefore said I, that he shall take of mine, and shall shew *it* unto you.

2 Timothy 2:7
Consider what I say; and the Lord give thee understanding in all things.

Can I discern good from evil?

1 John 4:6
We are of God: he that knoweth God heareth us; he that is not of God heareth not us. Hereby know we the spirit of truth, and the spirit of error.

1 John 4:1
Beloved, believe not every spirit, but try the spirits whether they are of God: because many false prophets are gone out into the world.

1 Thessalonians 5:21-22
Prove all things; hold fast that which is good. Abstain from all appearance of evil.

Ephesians 4:14
That we *henceforth* be no more children, tossed to and fro, and carried about with every wind of doctrine, by the sleight of men, *and* cunning craftiness, whereby they lie in wait to deceive.

ENCOURAGEMENT

How do I find encouragement?

2 Thessalonians 2:16-17

Now our Lord Jesus Christ himself, and God, even our Father, which hath loved us, and hath given us everlasting consolation and good hope through grace, Comfort your hearts, and stablish you in every good word and work.

Psalm 10:17

Lord, thou hast heard the desire of the humble: thou wilt prepare their heart, thou wilt cause thine ear to hear.

2 Corinthians 4:16

For which cause we faint not; but though our outward man perish, yet the inward man is renewed day by day.

Isaiah 43:1

But now thus saith the LORD that created thee, O Jacob, and he that formed thee, O Israel, Fear not: for I have redeemed thee, I have called *thee* by thy name; thou *art* mine.

Isaiah 41:10

Fear thou not; for I *am* with thee: be not dismayed; for I *am* thy God: I will strengthen thee; yea, I will help thee; yea, I will uphold thee with the right hand of my righteousness.

What should I do when I am discouraged?

Lamentations 3:25-26

The Lord *is* good unto them that wait for him, to the soul *that* seeketh him. *It is* good that *a man* should both hope and quietly wait for the salvation of the Lord.

Psalm 43:5

Why art thou cast down, O my soul? and why art thou disquieted within me? hope in God: for I shall yet praise him, *who is* the health of my countenance, and my God.

Psalm 55:22

Cast thy burden upon the Lord, and he shall sustain thee: he shall never suffer the righteous to be moved.

Hebrews 12:3

For consider him that endured such contradiction of sinners against himself, lest ye be wearied and faint in your minds.

2 Corinthians 13:4

For though he was crucified through weakness, yet he liveth by the power of God. For we also are weak in him, but we shall live with him by the power of God toward you.

How can I encourage others?

1 Thessalonians 5:11
Wherefore comfort yourselves together, and edify one another, even as also ye do.

Hebrews 3:12-13
Take heed, brethren, lest there be in any of you an evil heart of unbelief, in departing from the living God. But exhort one another daily, while it is called To day; lest any of you be hardened through the deceitfulness of sin.

1 Samuel 23:16
And Jonathan Saul's son arose, and went to David into the wood, and strengthened his hand in God.

Hebrews 10:24-25
And let us consider one another to provoke unto love and to good works: Not forsaking the assembling of ourselves together, as the manner of some *is;* but exhorting *one another:* and so much the more, as ye see the day approaching.

ETERNAL LIFE

What must I do to be saved?

Acts 16:31
And they said, Believe on the Lord Jesus Christ, and thou shalt be saved, and thy house.

Romans 10:9-10
That if thou shalt confess with thy mouth the Lord Jesus, and shalt believe in thine heart that God hath raised him from the dead, thou shalt be saved. For with the heart man believeth unto righteousness; and with the mouth confession is made unto salvation.

John 3:36
He that believeth on the Son hath everlasting life: and he that believeth not the Son shall not see life; but the wrath of God abideth on him.

1 John 5:11-12
And this is the record, that God hath given to us eternal life, and this life is in his Son. He that hath the Son hath life; *and* he that hath not the Son of God hath not life.

John 6:47
Verily, verily, I say unto you, He that believeth on me hath everlasting life.

Does God desire for anyone to perish?

1 Timothy 2:3-4
For this *is* good and acceptable in the sight of God our Saviour; Who will have all men to be saved, and to come unto the knowledge of the truth.

John 3:16
For God so loved the world, that he gave his only begotten Son, that whosoever believeth in him should not perish, but have everlasting life.

2 Peter 3:9
The Lord is not slack concerning his promise, as some men count slackness; but is longsuffering to us-ward, not willing that any should perish, but that all should come to repentance.

Luke 15:7
I say unto you, that likewise joy shall be in heaven over one sinner that repenteth, more than over ninety and nine just persons, which need no repentance.

Do I deserve eternal life?

Romans 6:23
For the wages of sin *is* death; but the gift of God *is* eternal life through Jesus Christ our Lord.

Titus 3:5
Not by works of righteousness which we have done, but according to his mercy he saved us, by the washing of regeneration, and renewing of the Holy Ghost.

Revelation 21:27
And there shall in no wise enter into it any thing that defileth, neither *whatsoever* worketh abomination, or *maketh* a lie: but they which are written in the Lamb's book of life.

Ephesians 2:8-10
For by grace are ye saved through faith; and that not of yourselves: *it is* the gift of God: Not of works, lest any man should boast. For we are his workmanship, created in Christ Jesus unto good works, which God hath before ordained that we should walk in them.

How does Jesus bless me with eternal life?

John 17:3
And this is life eternal, that they might know thee the only true God, and Jesus Christ, whom thou hast sent.

John 11:25-26
Jesus said unto her, I am the resurrection, and the life: he that believeth in me, though he were dead, yet shall he live: And whosoever liveth and believeth in me shall never die. Believest thou this?

John 20:29
Jesus saith unto him, Thomas, because thou hast seen me, thou hast believed: blessed *are* they that have not seen, and *yet* have believed.

1 John 2:17
And the world passeth away, and the lust thereof: but he that doeth the will of God abideth for ever.

Hebrews 5:9
And being made perfect, he became the author of eternal salvation unto all them that obey him.

FAITH

Should I put my faith in God?

Acts 16:31

And they said, Believe on the Lord Jesus Christ, and thou shalt be saved, and thy house.

Ephesians 2:8-9

For by grace are ye saved through faith; and that not of yourselves: *it is* the gift of God: Not of works, lest any man should boast.

Hebrews 11:1

Now faith is the substance of things hoped for, the evidence of things not seen.

1 Timothy 4:9-10

This *is* a faithful saying and worthy of all acceptation. For therefore we both labour and suffer reproach, because we trust in the living God, who is the Saviour of all men, specially of those that believe.

Romans 4:3

For what saith the scripture? Abraham believed God, and it was counted unto him for righteousness.

How powerful is faith in the Lord?

Matthew 17:20

And Jesus said unto them, Because of your unbelief: for verily I say unto you, If ye have faith as a grain of mustard seed, ye shall say unto this mountain, Remove hence to yonder place; and it shall remove; and nothing shall be impossible unto you.

John 14:12

Verily, verily, I say unto you, He that believeth on me, the works that I do shall he do also; and greater *works* than these shall he do; because I go unto my Father.

2 Corinthians 1:24

Not for that we have dominion over your faith, but are helpers of your joy: for by faith ye stand.

2 Corinthians 5:7

For we walk by faith, not by sight.

Does faith bring blessings for my life?

Isaiah 40:31
But they that wait upon the LORD shall renew *their* strength; they shall mount up with wings as eagles; they shall run, and not be weary; *and* they shall walk, and not faint.

Psalm 33:22
Let thy mercy, O LORD, be upon us, according as we hope in thee.

Romans 1:17
For therein is the righteousness of God revealed from faith to faith: as it is written, The just shall live by faith.

Romans 5:1-2
Therefore being justified by faith, we have peace with God through our Lord Jesus Christ: By whom also we have access by faith into this grace wherein we stand, and rejoice in hope of the glory of God.

Isaiah 26:3
Thou wilt keep *him* in perfect peace, *whose* mind *is* stayed *on thee:* because he trusteth in thee.

FORGIVENESS

What must I do to be forgiven?

Acts 10:43

To him give all the prophets witness, that through his name whosoever believeth in him shall receive remission of sins.

2 Chronicles 7:14

If my people, which are called by my name, shall humble themselves, and pray, and seek my face, and turn from their wicked ways; then will I hear from heaven, and will forgive their sin, and will heal their land.

1 John 1:9

If we confess our sins, he is faithful and just to forgive us *our* sins, and to cleanse us from all unrighteousness.

Isaiah 55:7

Let the wicked forsake his way, and the unrighteous man his thoughts: and let him return unto the LORD, and he will have mercy upon him; and to our God, for he will abundantly pardon.

Will God forgive me?

Colossians 2:13

And you, being dead in your sins and the uncircumcision of your flesh, hath he quickened together with him, having forgiven you all trespasses.

Psalm 51:7-9

Purge me with hyssop, and I shall be clean: wash me, and I shall be whiter than snow. Make me to hear joy and gladness; *that* the bones *which* thou hast broken may rejoice. Hide thy face from my sins, and blot out all mine iniquities.

Psalm 85:2

Thou hast forgiven the iniquity of thy people, thou hast covered all their sin. Selah.

Hebrews 8:12

For I will be merciful to their unrighteousness, and their sins and their iniquities will I remember no more.

Psalm 103:11-12

For as the heaven is high above the earth, *so* great is his mercy toward them that fear him. As far as the east is from the west, *so* far hath he removed our transgressions from us.

Isaiah 43:25

I, *even* I, *am* he that blotteth out thy transgressions for mine own sake, and will not remember thy sins.

Jeremiah 33:8

And I will cleanse them from all their iniquity, whereby they have sinned against me; and I will pardon all their iniquities, whereby they have sinned, and whereby they have transgressed against me.

Isaiah 1:18

Come now, and let us reason together, saith the LORD: though your sins be as scarlet, they shall be as white as snow; though they be red like crimson, they shall be as wool.

How does God forgive me?

Acts 13:38

Be it known unto you therefore, men *and* brethren, that through this man is preached unto you the forgiveness of sins.

Ephesians 1:6-7

To the praise of the glory of his grace, wherein he hath made us accepted in the beloved. In whom we have redemption through his blood, the forgiveness of sins, according to the riches of his grace.

Romans 8:1

There is therefore now no condemnation to them which are in Christ Jesus, who walk not after the flesh, but after the Spirit.

1 Peter 2:24

Who his own self bare our sins in his own body on the tree, that we, being dead to sins, should live unto righteousness: by whose stripes ye were healed.

Matthew 26:28

For this is my blood of the new testament, which is shed for many for the remission of sins.

Why should I forgive others?

Colossians 3:13
Forbearing one another, and forgiving one another, if any man have a quarrel against any: even as Christ forgave you, so also *do* ye.

Luke 23:34
Then said Jesus, Father, forgive them; for they know not what they do.

Luke 6:36
Be ye therefore merciful, as your Father also is merciful.

Luke 6:37
Judge not, and ye shall not be judged: condemn not, and ye shall not be condemned: forgive, and ye shall be forgiven.

Matthew 6:14-15
For if ye forgive men their trespasses, your heavenly Father will also forgive you: But if ye forgive not men their trespasses, neither will your Father forgive your trespasses.

How should I forgive others?

Ephesians 4:32

And be ye kind one to another, tenderhearted, forgiving one another, even as God for Christ's sake hath forgiven you.

Luke 17:3

Take heed to yourselves: If thy brother trespass against thee, rebuke him; and if he repent, forgive him.

Matthew 18:21-22

Then came Peter to him, and said, Lord, how oft shall my brother sin against me, and I forgive him? till seven times? Jesus saith unto him, I say not unto thee, Until seven times: but, Until seventy times seven.

Romans 12:20-21

Therefore if thine enemy hunger, feed him; if he thirst, give him drink: for in so doing thou shalt heap coals of fire on his head. Be not overcome of evil, but overcome evil with good.

1 Peter 3:9

Not rendering evil for evil, or railing for railing: but contrariwise blessing; knowing that ye are thereunto called, that ye should inherit a blessing.

Luke 6:27

But I say unto you which hear, Love your enemies, do good to them which hate you.

Romans 12:14

Bless them which persecute you: bless, and curse not.

Matthew 5:23-24

Therefore if thou bring thy gift to the altar, and there rememberest that thy brother hath ought against thee; Leave there thy gift before the altar, and go thy way; first be reconciled to thy brother, and then come and offer thy gift.

Matthew 6:12

And forgive us our debts, as we forgive our debtors.

FREEDOM

Is true freedom found in forgiveness?

Matthew 26:28
For this is my blood of the new testament, which is shed for many for the remission of sins.

Psalm 130:4
But *there is* forgiveness with thee, that thou mayest be feared.

Acts 2:38
Then Peter said unto them, Repent, and be baptized every one of you in the name of Jesus Christ for the remission of sins, and ye shall receive the gift of the Holy Ghost.

Acts 10:43
To him give all the prophets witness, that through his name whosoever believeth in him shall receive remission of sins.

Acts 13:38
Be it known unto you therefore, men *and* brethren, that through this man is preached unto you the forgiveness of sins.

Can I live as a free man or woman?

2 Corinthians 3:17

Now the Lord is that Spirit: and where the Spirit of the Lord *is,* there *is* liberty.

Galatians 5:1

Stand fast therefore in the liberty wherewith Christ hath made us free, and be not entangled again with the yoke of bondage.

Galatians 5:13

For, brethren, ye have been called unto liberty; only *use* not liberty for an occasion to the flesh, but by love serve one another.

Ephesians 3:12

In whom we have boldness and access with confidence by the faith of him.

1 Peter 2:16

As free, and not using *your* liberty for a cloke of maliciousness, but as the servants of God.

FRIENDSHIP

What are the marks of true friendship?

Proverbs 17:17
A friend loveth at all times, and a brother is born for adversity.

Genesis 50:21
Now therefore fear ye not: I will nourish you, and your little ones. And he comforted them, and spake kindly unto them.

John 13:14-15
If I then, *your* Lord and Master, have washed your feet; ye also ought to wash one another's feet. For I have given you an example, that ye should do as I have done to you.

Proverbs 18:24
A man *that hath* friends must shew himself friendly: and there is a friend *that* sticketh closer than a brother.

John 15:13
Greater love hath no man than this, that a man lay down his life for his friends.

What is the purpose of friendship?

Ecclesiastes 4:9

Two *are* better than one; because they have a good reward for their labour.

Ecclesiastes 4:10

For if they fall, the one will lift up his fellow: but woe to him *that is* alone when he falleth; for *he hath* not another to help him up.

1 Thessalonians 2:11-12

As ye know how we exhorted and comforted and charged every one of you, as a father *doth* his children, That ye would walk worthy of God, who hath called you unto his kingdom and glory.

Acts 2:42

And they continued stedfastly in the apostles' doctrine and fellowship, and in breaking of bread, and in prayers.

Matthew 18:20

For where two or three are gathered together in my name, there am I in the midst of them.

Who are some great friends in the Bible?

1 Samuel 18:1

And it came to pass, when he had made an end of speaking unto Saul, that the soul of Jonathan was knit with the soul of David, and Jonathan loved him as his own soul.

1 Samuel 18:3

Then Jonathan and David made a covenant, because he loved him as his own soul.

Ruth 1:16

And Ruth said, Intreat me not to leave thee, *or* to return from following after thee: for whither thou goest, I will go; and where thou lodgest, I will lodge: thy people *shall be* my people, and thy God my God.

Daniel 2:17-18

Then Daniel went to his house, and made the thing known to Hananiah, Mishael, and Azariah, his companions: That they would desire mercies of the God of heaven concerning this secret; that Daniel and his fellows should not perish with the rest of the wise *men* of Babylon.

Luke 8:1-3

And it came to pass afterward, that he went throughout every city and village, preaching and shewing the glad tidings of the kingdom of God: and the twelve *were* with him, And certain women, which had been healed of evil spirits and infirmities, Mary called Magdalene, out of whom went seven devils, And Joanna the wife of Chuza Herod's steward, and Susanna, and many others, which ministered unto him of their substance.

How can I make strong friendships?

1 Peter 4:8
And above all things have fervent charity among yourselves: for charity shall cover the multitude of sins.

Psalm 119:63
I *am* a companion of all *them* that fear thee, and of them that keep thy precepts.

Luke 6:31
And as ye would that men should do to you, do ye also to them likewise.

Proverbs 13:20
He that walketh with wise *men* shall be wise: but a companion of fools shall be destroyed.

Proverbs 22:24-25
Make no friendship with an angry man; and with a furious man thou shalt not go: Lest thou learn his ways, and get a snare to thy soul.

Colossians 3:14
And above all these things *put on* charity, which is the bond of perfectness.

What ruins friendships?

1 Samuel 18:8-10, 12

And Saul was very wroth, and the saying displeased him; and he said, They have ascribed unto David ten thousands, and to me they have ascribed but thousands: and what can he have more but the kingdom? And Saul eyed David from that day and forward. And it came to pass on the morrow, that the evil spirit from God came upon Saul...And Saul was afraid of David, because the Lord was with him, and was departed from Saul.

1 Corinthians 13:4-7

Charity suffereth long, and is kind; charity envieth not; charity vaunteth not itself, is not puffed up, Doth not behave itself unseemly, seeketh not her own, is not easily provoked, thinketh no evil; Rejoiceth not in iniquity, but rejoiceth in the truth; Beareth all things, believeth all things, hopeth all things, endureth all things.

Philippians 2:3-4

Let nothing be done through strife or vainglory; but in lowliness of mind let each esteem other better than themselves. Look not every man on his own things, but every man also on the things of others.

Proverbs 17:9

He that covereth a transgression seeketh love; but he that repeateth a matter separateth *very* friends.

Job 17:5

He that speaketh flattery to *his* friends, even the eyes of his children shall fail.

GIVING

Who should I give to?

Leviticus 27:30-32

And all the tithe of the land, whether of the seed of the land, or of the fruit of the tree, is the Lord's: it is holy unto the Lord. And if a man will at all redeem ought of his tithes, he shall add thereto the fifth part thereof. And concerning the tithe of the herd, or of the flock, even of whatsoever passeth under the rod, the tenth shall be holy unto the Lord.

1 John 3:17-18

But whoso hath this world's good, and seeth his brother have need, and shutteth up his bowels of compassion from him, how dwelleth the love of God in him? My little children, let us not love in word, neither in tongue; but in deed and in truth.

Romans 12:10,13

Be kindly affectioned one to another with brotherly love; in honour preferring one another; Distributing to the necessity of saints; given to hospitality.

Deuteronomy 15:7-8, 10-11

If there be among you a poor man of one of thy brethren within any of thy gates in thy land which the Lord thy God giveth thee, thou shalt not harden thine heart, nor shut thine hand from thy poor brother: But thou shalt open thine hand wide unto him, and shalt surely lend him sufficient for his need, in that which he wanteth. Thou shalt surely give him, and thine heart shall not be grieved when thou givest unto him: because that for this thing the Lord thy God shall bless thee in all thy works, and in all that thou puttest thine hand unto. For the poor shall never cease out of the land: therefore I command thee, saying, Thou shalt open thine hand wide unto thy brother, to thy poor, and to thy needy, in thy land.

Ephesians 4:28

Let him that stole steal no more: but rather let him labour, working with his hands the thing which is good, that he may have to give to him that needeth.

How should I give?

Matthew 6:1-4

Take heed that ye do not your alms before men, to be seen of them: otherwise ye have no reward of your Father which is in heaven. Therefore when thou doest thine alms, do not sound a trumpet before thee, as the hypocrites do in the synagogues and in the streets, that they may have glory of men. Verily I say unto you, They have their reward. But when thou doest alms, let not thy left hand know what thy right hand doeth: That thine alms may be in secret: and thy Father which seeth in secret himself shall reward thee openly.

2 Corinthians 9:6-7

But this I say, He which soweth sparingly shall reap also sparingly; and he which soweth bountifully shall reap also bountifully. Every man according as he purposeth in his heart, so let him give; not grudgingly, or of necessity: for God loveth a cheerful giver.

Acts 20:35

I have shewed you all things, how that so labouring ye ought to support the weak, and to remember the words of the Lord Jesus, how he said, It is more blessed to give than to receive.

What are some examples of giving?

Philippians 4:10-11, 14-19

But I rejoiced in the Lord greatly, that now at the last your care of me hath flourished again; wherein ye were also careful, but ye lacked opportunity. Not that I speak in respect of want: for I have learned, in whatsoever state I am, therewith to be content. Notwithstanding ye have well done, that ye did communicate with my affliction. Now ye Philippians know also, that in the beginning of the gospel, when I departed from Macedonia, no church communicated with me as concerning giving and receiving, but ye only. For even in Thessalonica ye sent once and again unto my necessity. Not because I desire a gift: but I desire fruit that may abound to your account. But I have all, and abound: I am full, having received of Epaphroditus the things which were sent from you, an odour of a sweet smell, a sacrifice acceptable, wellpleasing to God. But my God shall supply all your need according to his riches in glory by Christ Jesus.

Acts 2:44-45

And all that believed were together, and had all things common; And sold their possessions and goods, and parted them to all men, as every man had need.

Acts 4:32-37

And the multitude of them that believed were of one heart and of one soul: neither said any of them that ought of the things which he possessed was his own; but they had all things common. And with great power gave the apostles witness of the resurrection of the Lord Jesus: and great grace was upon them all. Neither was there any among them that lacked: for as many as were possessors of lands or houses sold them, and brought the prices of the things that were sold, And laid them down at the apostles' feet: and distribution was made unto every man according as he had need. And Joses, who by the apostles was surnamed Barnabas, (which is, being interpreted, The son of consolation,) a Levite, and of the country of Cyprus, Having land, sold it, and brought the money, and laid it at the apostles' feet.

GOD'S WILL

Is it possible to know God's will?

Philippians 2:13
For it is God which worketh in you both to will and to do of his good pleasure.

Proverbs 3:5-6
Trust in the Lord with all thine heart; and lean not unto thine own understanding. In all thy ways acknowledge him, and he shall direct thy paths.

Proverbs 2:3-5
Yea, if thou criest after knowledge, and liftest up thy voice for understanding; If thou seekest her as silver, and searchest for her as for hid treasures; Then shalt thou understand the fear of the Lord, and find the knowledge of God.

Romans 12:2
And be not conformed to this world: but be ye transformed by the renewing of your mind, that ye may prove what is that good, and acceptable, and perfect, will of God.

John 8:31-32
Then said Jesus to those Jews which believed on him, If ye continue in my word, then are ye my disciples indeed; And ye shall know the truth, and the truth shall make you free.

Psalm 37:23
The steps of a good man are ordered by the Lord: and he delighteth in his way.

What is God's will for me?

Micah 6:8

He hath shewed thee, O man, what is good; and what doth the Lord require of thee, but to do justly, and to love mercy, and to walk humbly with thy God?

1 Peter 2:15

For so is the will of God, that with well doing ye may put to silence the ignorance of foolish men.

Ephesians 5:17-18

Wherefore be ye not unwise, but understanding what the will of the Lord is. And be not drunk with wine, wherein is excess; but be filled with the Spirit.

1 Thessalonians 4:3

For this is the will of God, even your sanctification, that ye should abstain from fornication.

1 Peter 4:19

Wherefore let them that suffer according to the will of God commit the keeping of their souls to him in well doing, as unto a faithful Creator.

1 Thessalonians 5:18

In every thing give thanks: for this is the will of God in Christ Jesus concerning you.

How should I respond to God's will?

Psalm 40:8
I delight to do thy will, O my God: yea, thy law is within my heart.

Psalm 143:10
Teach me to do thy will; for thou art my God: thy spirit is good; lead me into the land of uprightness.

Acts 21:14
And when he would not be persuaded, we ceased, saying, The will of the Lord be done.

Ephesians 6:6
Not with eyeservice, as menpleasers; but as the servants of Christ, doing the will of God from the heart.

Matthew 12:50
For whosoever shall do the will of my Father which is in heaven, the same is my brother, and sister, and mother.

James 4:15
For that ye ought to say, If the Lord will, we shall live, and do this, or that.

GRACE

What does God's grace look like?

John 1:14-18

And the Word was made flesh, and dwelt among us, (and we beheld his glory, the glory as of the only begotten of the Father,) full of grace and truth.

John bare witness of him, and cried, saying, This was he of whom I spake, He that cometh after me is preferred before me: for he was before me. And of his fulness have all we received, and grace for grace. For the law was given by Moses, but grace and truth came by Jesus Christ. No man hath seen God at any time; the only begotten Son, which is in the bosom of the Father, he hath declared him.

Romans 5:1-2

Therefore being justified by faith, we have peace with God through our Lord Jesus Christ: By whom also we have access by faith into this grace wherein we stand, and rejoice in hope of the glory of God.

How is God's grace revealed in salvation?

Ephesians 2:4-9

But God, who is rich in mercy, for his great love wherewith he loved us, Even when we were dead in sins, hath quickened us together with Christ, (by grace ye are saved;) And hath raised us up together, and made us sit together in heavenly places in Christ Jesus: That in the ages to come he might shew the exceeding riches of his grace in his kindness toward us through Christ Jesus. For by grace are ye saved through faith; and that not of yourselves: it is the gift of God: Not of works, lest any man should boast.

Acts 15:11

But we believe that through the grace of the Lord Jesus Christ we shall be saved, even as they.

Ephesians 1:3-7

Blessed be the God and Father of our Lord Jesus Christ, who hath blessed us with all spiritual blessings in heavenly places in Christ: According as he hath chosen us in him before the foundation of the world, that we should be holy and without blame before him in love: Having predestinated us unto the adoption of children by Jesus Christ to himself, according to the good pleasure of his will, To the praise of the glory of his grace, wherein he hath made us accepted in the beloved. In whom we have redemption through his blood, the forgiveness of sins, according to the riches of his grace.

How should this grace impact my life each day?

Titus 2:11-13

For the grace of God that bringeth salvation hath appeared to all men, Teaching us that, denying ungodliness and worldly lusts, we should live soberly, righteously, and godly, in this present world; Looking for that blessed hope, and the glorious appearing of the great God and our Saviour Jesus Christ.

2 Corinthians 9:8

And God is able to make all grace abound toward you; that ye, always having all sufficiency in all things, may abound to every good work.

1 Peter 1:13

Wherefore gird up the loins of your mind, be sober, and hope to the end for the grace that is to be brought unto you at the revelation of Jesus Christ.

2 Corinthians 12:7-10

And lest I should be exalted above measure through the abundance of the revelations, there was given to me a thorn in the flesh, the messenger of Satan to buffet me, lest I should be exalted above measure. For this thing I besought the Lord thrice, that it might depart from me. And he said unto me, My grace is sufficient for thee: for my strength is made perfect in weakness. Most gladly therefore will I rather glory in my infirmities, that the power of Christ may rest upon me. Therefore I take pleasure in infirmities, in reproaches, in necessities, in persecutions, in distresses for Christ's sake: for when I am weak, then am I strong.

Hebrews 4:15-16

For we have not an high priest which cannot be touched with the feeling of our infirmities; but was in all points tempted like as we are, yet without sin. Let us therefore come boldly unto the throne of grace, that we may obtain mercy, and find grace to help in time of need.

Colossians 4:5-6

Walk in wisdom toward them that are without, redeeming the time. Let your speech be alway with grace, seasoned with salt, that ye may know how ye ought to answer every man.

Hebrews 12:14-15

Follow peace with all men, and holiness, without which no man shall see the Lord: Looking diligently lest any man fail of the grace of God; lest any root of bitterness springing up trouble you, and thereby many be defiled.

James 4:6

But he giveth more grace. Wherefore he saith, God resisteth the proud, but giveth grace unto the humble.

1 Peter 5:5-6

. . . Yea, all of you be subject one to another, and be clothed with humility: for God resisteth the proud, and giveth grace to the humble. Humble yourselves therefore under the mighty hand of God, that he may exalt you in due time.

1 Peter 4:10-11

As every man hath received the gift, even so minister the same one to another, as good stewards of the manifold grace of God. If any man speak, let him speak as the oracles of God; if any man minister, let him do it as of the ability which God giveth: that God in all things may be glorified through Jesus Christ, to whom be praise and dominion for ever and ever. Amen.

HEAVEN

What is heaven like?

Isaiah 66:1

Thus saith the Lord, The heaven is my throne, and the earth is my footstool: where is the house that ye build unto me? and where is the place of my rest?

Revelation 4:3-4, 6

And he that sat was to look upon like a jasper and a sardine stone: and there was a rainbow round about the throne, in sight like unto an emerald. And round about the throne were four and twenty seats: and upon the seats I saw four and twenty elders sitting, clothed in white raiment; and they had on their heads crowns of gold... And before the throne there was a sea of glass like unto crystal...

Revelation 4:8-11

...They rest not day and night, saying, Holy, holy, holy, Lord God Almighty, which was, and is, and is to come. And when those beasts give glory and honour and thanks to him that sat on the throne, who liveth for ever and ever, The four and twenty elders fall down before him that sat on the throne, and worship him that liveth for ever and ever, and cast their crowns before the throne, saying, Thou art worthy, O Lord, to receive glory and honour and power: for thou hast created all things, and for thy pleasure they are and were created.

Revelation 5:11-14

And the number of them was ten thousand times ten thousand, and thousands of thousands; Saying with a loud voice, Worthy is the Lamb that was slain to receive power, and riches, and wisdom, and strength, and honour, and glory, and blessing. And every creature which is in heaven, and on the earth, and under the earth, and such as are in the sea, and all that are in them, heard I saying, Blessing, and honour, and glory, and power, be unto him that sitteth upon the throne, and unto the Lamb for ever and ever.

Revelation 21:1-4

And I saw a new heaven and a new earth: for the first heaven and the first earth were passed away; and there was no more sea. And I John saw the holy city, new Jerusalem, coming down from God out of heaven, prepared as a bride adorned for her husband. And I heard a great voice out of heaven saying, Behold, the tabernacle of God is with men, and he will dwell with them, and they shall be his people, and God himself shall be with them, and be their God. And God shall wipe away all tears from their eyes; and there shall be no more death, neither sorrow, nor crying, neither shall there be any more pain: for the former things are passed away.

Revelation 21:18-19, 21-23

And the building of the wall of it was of jasper: and the city was pure gold, like unto clear glass. And the foundations of the wall of the city were garnished with all manner of precious stones...And the twelve gates were twelve pearls; every several gate was of one pearl: and the street of the city was pure gold, as it were transparent glass. And I saw no temple therein: for the Lord God Almighty and the Lamb are the temple of it. And the city had no need of the sun, neither of the moon, to shine in it: for the glory of God did lighten it, and the Lamb is the light thereof.

Revelation 22:1-5

And he shewed me a pure river of water of life, clear as crystal, proceeding out of the throne of God and of the Lamb. In the midst of the street of it, and on either side of the river, was there the tree of life, which bare twelve manner of fruits, and yielded her fruit every month: and the leaves of the tree were for the healing of the nations. And there shall be no more curse: but the throne of God and of the Lamb shall be in it; and his servants shall serve him: And they shall see his face; and his name shall be in their foreheads. And there shall be no night there; and they need no candle, neither light of the sun; for the Lord God giveth them light: and they shall reign for ever and ever.

Who will be in heaven?

Matthew 18:2-5

And Jesus called a little child unto him, and set him in the midst of them, And said, Verily I say unto you, Except ye be converted, and become as little children, ye shall not enter into the kingdom of heaven. Whosoever therefore shall humble himself as this little child, the same is greatest in the kingdom of heaven. And whoso shall receive one such little child in my name receiveth me.

1 Peter 1:3-5

Blessed be the God and Father of our Lord Jesus Christ, which according to his abundant mercy hath begotten us again unto a lively hope by the resurrection of Jesus Christ from the dead, To an inheritance incorruptible, and undefiled, and that fadeth not away, reserved in heaven for you, Who are kept by the power of God through faith unto salvation ready to be revealed in the last time.

Matthew 10:32-33

Whosoever therefore shall confess me before men, him will I confess also before my Father which is in heaven. But whosoever shall deny me before men, him will I also deny before my Father which is in heaven.

Matthew 7:21-23

Not every one that saith unto me, Lord, Lord, shall enter into the kingdom of heaven; but he that doeth the will of my Father which is in heaven. Many will say to me in that day, Lord, Lord, have we not prophesied in thy name? and in thy name have cast out devils? and in thy name done many wonderful works? And then will I profess unto them, I never knew you: depart from me, ye that work iniquity.

Matthew 25:31-40

And he shall separate them one from another, as a shepherd divideth his sheep from the goats: And he shall set the sheep on his right hand, but the goats on the left. Then shall the King say unto them on his right hand, Come, ye blessed of my Father, inherit the kingdom prepared for you from the foundation of the world: For I was an hungred, and ye gave me meat: I was thirsty, and ye gave me drink: I was a stranger, and ye took me in: Naked, and ye clothed me: I was sick, and ye visited me: I was in prison, and ye came unto me. Then shall the righteous answer him, saying, Lord, when saw we thee an hungred, and fed thee? or thirsty, and gave thee drink? When saw we thee a stranger, and took thee in? or naked, and clothed thee? Or when saw we thee sick, or in prison, and came unto thee? And the King shall answer and say unto them, Verily I say unto you, Inasmuch as ye have done it unto one of the least of these my brethren, ye have done it unto me.

Revelation 21:6-8

And he said unto me, It is done. I am Alpha and Omega, the beginning and the end. I will give unto him that is athirst of the fountain of the water of life freely. He that overcometh shall inherit all things; and I will be his God, and he shall be my son. But the fearful, and unbelieving, and the abominable, and murderers, and whoremongers, and sorcerers, and idolaters, and all liars, shall have their part in the lake which burneth with fire and brimstone: which is the second death.

Revelation 21:27

And there shall in no wise enter into it any thing that defileth, neither whatsoever worketh abomination, or maketh a lie: but they which are written in the Lamb's book of life.

How do I prepare for heaven?

John 14:1-7

Let not your heart be troubled: ye believe in God, believe also in me. In my Father's house are many mansions: if it were not so, I would have told you. I go to prepare a place for you. And if I go and prepare a place for you, I will come again, and receive you unto myself; that where I am, there ye may be also. And whither I go ye know, and the way ye know. Thomas saith unto him, Lord, we know not whither thou goest; and how can we know the way? Jesus saith unto him, I am the way, the truth, and the life: no man cometh unto the Father, but by me. If ye had known me, ye should have known my Father also: and from henceforth ye know him, and have seen him.

Colossians 3:1-4

If ye then be risen with Christ, seek those things which are above, where Christ sitteth on the right hand of God. Set your affection on things above, not on things on the earth. For ye are dead, and your life is hid with Christ in God. When Christ, who is our life, shall appear, then shall ye also appear with him in glory.

Matthew 6:19-21

Lay not up for yourselves treasures upon earth, where moth and rust doth corrupt, and where thieves break through and steal: But lay up for yourselves treasures in heaven, where neither moth nor rust doth corrupt, and where thieves do not break through nor steal: For where your treasure is, there will your heart be also.

1 Peter 1:13
Wherefore gird up the loins of your mind, be sober, and hope to the end for the grace that is to be brought unto you at the revelation of Jesus Christ.

What did Jesus say the kingdom of heaven is like?

Matthew 13:31-33

Another parable put he forth unto them, saying, The kingdom of heaven is like to a grain of mustard seed, which a man took, and sowed in his field: Which indeed is the least of all seeds: but when it is grown, it is the greatest among herbs, and becometh a tree, so that the birds of the air come and lodge in the branches thereof.

Another parable spake he unto them; The kingdom of heaven is like unto leaven, which a woman took, and hid in three measures of meal, till the whole was leavened.

Matthew 13:44-49

Again, the kingdom of heaven is like unto treasure hid in a field; the which when a man hath found, he hideth, and for joy thereof goeth and selleth all that he hath, and buyeth that field.

Again, the kingdom of heaven is like unto a merchant man, seeking goodly pearls: Who, when he had found one pearl of great price, went and sold all that he had, and bought it.

Again, the kingdom of heaven is like unto a net, that was cast into the sea, and gathered of every kind: Which, when it was full, they drew to shore, and sat down, and gathered the good into vessels, but cast the bad away. So shall it be at the end of the world: the angels shall come forth, and sever the wicked from among the just.

Matthew 18:23-35

Therefore is the kingdom of heaven likened unto a certain king, which would take account of his servants. And when he had begun to reckon, one was brought unto him, which owed him ten thousand talents. But forasmuch as he had not to pay, his lord commanded him to be sold, and his wife, and children, and all that he had, and payment to be made. The servant therefore fell down, and worshipped him, saying, Lord, have patience with me, and I will pay thee all. Then the lord of that servant was moved with compassion, and loosed him, and forgave him the debt. But the same servant went out, and found one of his fellowservants, which owed him an hundred pence: and he laid hands on him, and took him by the throat, saying, Pay me that thou owest. And his fellowservant fell down at his feet, and besought him, saying, Have patience with me, and I will pay thee all. And he would not: but went and cast him into prison, till he should pay the debt. So when his fellowservants saw what was done, they were very sorry, and came and told unto their lord all that was done. Then his lord, after that he had called him, said unto him, O thou wicked servant, I forgave thee all that debt, because thou desiredst me: Shouldest not thou also have had compassion on thy fellowservant, even as I had pity on thee? And his lord was wroth, and delivered him to the tormentors, till he should pay all that was due unto him. So likewise shall my heavenly Father do also unto you, if ye from your hearts forgive not every one his brother their trespasses.

Matthew 20:1-16

For the kingdom of heaven is like unto a man that is an householder, which went out early in the morning to hire labourers into his vineyard. And when he had agreed with the labourers for a penny a day, he sent them into his vineyard. And he went out about the third hour, and saw others standing idle in the marketplace, And said unto them; Go ye also into the vineyard, and whatsoever is right I will give you. And they went their way. Again he went out about the sixth and ninth hour, and did likewise. And about the eleventh hour he went out, and found others standing idle, and saith unto them, Why stand ye here all the day idle? They say unto him, Because no man hath hired us. He saith unto them, Go ye also into the vineyard; and whatsoever is right, that shall ye receive. So when even was come, the lord of the vineyard saith unto his steward, Call the labourers, and give them their hire, beginning from the last unto the first. And when they came that were hired about the eleventh hour, they received every man a penny. But when the first came, they supposed that they should have received more; and they likewise received every man a penny. And when they had received it, they murmured against the goodman of the house, Saying, These last have wrought but one hour, and thou hast made them equal unto us, which have borne the burden and heat of the day. But he answered one of them, and said, Friend, I do thee no wrong: didst not thou agree with me for a penny? Take that thine is, and go thy way: I will give unto this last, even as unto thee. Is it not lawful for me to do what I will with mine own? Is thine eye evil, because I am good? So the last shall be first, and the first last: for many be called, but few chosen.

Matthew 25:1-13

Then shall the kingdom of heaven be likened unto ten virgins, which took their lamps, and went forth to meet the bridegroom. And five of them were wise, and five were foolish. They that were foolish took their lamps, and took no oil with them: But the wise took oil in their vessels with their lamps. While the bridegroom tarried, they all slumbered and slept. And at midnight there was a cry made, Behold, the bridegroom cometh; go ye out to meet him. Then all those virgins arose, and trimmed their lamps. And the foolish said unto the wise, Give us of your oil; for our lamps are gone out. But the wise answered, saying,

Not so; lest there be not enough for us and you: but go ye rather to them that sell, and buy for yourselves. And while they went to buy, the bridegroom came; and they that were ready went in with him to the marriage: and the door was shut. Afterward came also the other virgins, saying, Lord, Lord, open to us. But he answered and said, Verily I say unto you, I know you not. Watch therefore, for ye know neither the day nor the hour wherein the Son of man cometh.

Matthew 25:14-30

For the kingdom of heaven is as a man travelling into a far country, who called his own servants, and delivered unto them his goods. And unto one he gave five talents, to another two, and to another one; to every man according to his several ability; and straightway took his journey. Then he that had received the five talents went and traded with the same, and made them other five talents. And likewise he that had received two, he also gained other two. But he that had received one went and digged in the earth, and hid his lord's money. After a long time the lord of those servants cometh, and reckoneth with them. And so he that had received five talents came and brought other five talents, saying, Lord, thou deliveredst unto me five talents: behold, I have gained beside them five talents more. His lord said unto him, Well done, thou good and faithful servant: thou hast been faithful over a few things, I will make thee ruler over many things: enter thou into the joy of thy lord. He also that had received two talents came and said, Lord, thou deliveredst unto me two talents: behold, I have gained two other talents beside them. His lord said unto him, Well done, good and faithful servant; thou hast been faithful over a few things, I will make thee ruler over many things: enter thou into the joy of thy lord. Then he which had received the one talent came and said, Lord, I knew thee that thou art an hard man, reaping where thou hast not sown, and gathering where thou hast not strawed: And I was afraid, and went and hid thy talent in the earth: lo, there thou hast that is thine. His lord answered and said unto him, Thou wicked and slothful servant, thou knewest that I reap where I sowed not, and gather where I have not strawed: Thou oughtest therefore to have put my money to the exchangers, and then at my coming I should have received mine own with usury. Take therefore the talent from him, and give it unto him which hath ten talents. For unto every one that hath shall be given, and he shall have abundance: but from him that hath not shall be taken away even that which he hath. And cast ye the unprofitable servant into outer darkness: there shall be weeping and gnashing of teeth.

HOLINESS

Is God holy?

1 Samuel 2:2
There is none holy as the Lord: for there is none beside thee: neither is there any rock like our God.

Isaiah 6:1-3
In the year that king Uzziah died I saw also the Lord sitting upon a throne, high and lifted up, and his train filled the temple. Above it stood the seraphims: each one had six wings; with twain he covered his face, and with twain he covered his feet, and with twain he did fly. And one cried unto another, and said, Holy, holy, holy, is the Lord of hosts: the whole earth is full of his glory.

Exodus 15:11
Who is like unto thee, O Lord, among the gods? who is like thee, glorious in holiness, fearful in praises, doing wonders?

Psalm 99:1-3
The Lord reigneth; let the people tremble: he sitteth between the cherubims; let the earth be moved. The Lord is great in Zion; and he is high above all the people. Let them praise thy great and terrible name; for it is holy.

How should I respond to God's holiness?

1 Chronicles 16:29
Give unto the Lord the glory due unto his name: bring an offering, and come before him: worship the Lord in the beauty of holiness.

1 Peter 1:14-16
As obedient children, not fashioning yourselves according to the former lusts in your ignorance: But as he which hath called you is holy, so be ye holy in all manner of conversation; Because it is written, Be ye holy; for I am holy.

1 Thessalonians 4:7
For God hath not called us unto uncleanness, but unto holiness.

Leviticus 11:44-45
For I am the Lord your God: ye shall therefore sanctify yourselves, and ye shall be holy; for I am holy: neither shall ye defile yourselves with any manner of creeping thing that creepeth upon the earth. For I am the Lord that bringeth you up out of the land of Egypt, to be your God: ye shall therefore be holy, for I am holy.

Leviticus 20:7-8
Sanctify yourselves therefore, and be ye holy: for I am

the Lord your God. And ye shall keep my statutes, and do them: I am the Lord which sanctify you.

HOLY SPIRIT

Who is the Holy Spirit?

Isaiah 11:2
And the spirit of the Lord shall rest upon him, the spirit of wisdom and understanding, the spirit of counsel and might, the spirit of knowledge and of the fear of the Lord.

Genesis 1:2
And the earth was without form, and void; and darkness was upon the face of the deep. And the Spirit of God moved upon the face of the waters.

Nehemiah 9:20
Thou gavest also thy good spirit to instruct them, and withheldest not thy manna from their mouth, and gavest them water for their thirst.

Romans 5:5
And hope maketh not ashamed; because the love of God is shed abroad in our hearts by the Holy Ghost which is given unto us.

1 Peter 1:11
Searching what, or what manner of time the Spirit of Christ which was in them did signify, when it testified beforehand the sufferings of Christ, and the glory that should follow.

John 15:26
But when the Comforter is come, whom I will send unto you from the Father, even the Spirit of truth, which proceedeth from the Father, he shall testify of me.

John 16:7
Nevertheless I tell you the truth; It is expedient for you that I go away: for if I go not away, the Comforter will not come unto you; but if I depart, I will send him unto you.

John 14:16-17
And I will pray the Father, and he shall give you another Comforter, that he may abide with you for ever; Even the Spirit of truth; whom the world cannot receive, because it seeth him not, neither knoweth him: but ye know him; for he dwelleth with you, and shall be in you.

How has the Holy Spirit acted in the past?

Job 33:4
The Spirit of God hath made me, and the breath of the Almighty hath given me life.

2 Peter 1:21
For the prophecy came not in old time by the will of man: but holy men of God spake as they were moved by the Holy Ghost.

Hebrews 9:14
How much more shall the blood of Christ, who through the eternal Spirit offered himself without spot to God, purge your conscience from dead works to serve the living God?

Romans 8:11
But if the Spirit of him that raised up Jesus from the dead dwell in you, he that raised up Christ from the dead shall also quicken your mortal bodies by his Spirit that dwelleth in you.

Matthew 3:16
And Jesus, when he was baptized, went up straightway out of the water: and, lo, the heavens were opened unto him, and he saw the Spirit of God descending like a dove, and lighting upon him.

Acts 1:5
For John truly baptized with water; but ye shall be baptized with the Holy Ghost not many days hence.

1 Peter 1:2
Elect according to the foreknowledge of God the Father, through sanctification of the Spirit, unto obedience and sprinkling of the blood of Jesus Christ: Grace unto you, and peace, be multiplied.

What is the Holy Spirit doing now?

1 Corinthians 2:10
But God hath revealed them unto us by his Spirit: for the Spirit searcheth all things, yea, the deep things of God.

John 14:26
But the Comforter, which is the Holy Ghost, whom the Father will send in my name, he shall teach you all things, and bring all things to your remembrance, whatsoever I have said unto you.

John 16:8
And when he is come, he will reprove the world of sin, and of righteousness, and of judgment.

Ezekiel 36:27
And I will put my spirit within you, and cause you to walk in my statutes, and ye shall keep my judgments, and do them.

Romans 15:16
That I should be the minister of Jesus Christ to the Gentiles, ministering the gospel of God, that the offering up of the Gentiles might be acceptable, being sanctified by the Holy Ghost.

Titus 3:5

Not by works of righteousness which we have done, but according to his mercy he saved us, by the washing of regeneration, and renewing of the Holy Ghost.

1 Corinthians 12:11

But all these worketh that one and the selfsame Spirit, dividing to every man severally as he will.

Acts 1:8

But ye shall receive power, after that the Holy Ghost is come upon you: and ye shall be witnesses unto me both in Jerusalem, and in all Judaea, and in Samaria, and unto the uttermost part of the earth.

Isaiah 30:21

And thine ears shall hear a word behind thee, saying, This is the way, walk ye in it, when ye turn to the right hand, and when ye turn to the left.

Mark 13:11

But when they shall lead you, and deliver you up, take no thought beforehand what ye shall speak, neither do ye premeditate: but whatsoever shall be given you in that hour, that speak ye: for it is not ye that speak, but the Holy Ghost.

Do all Christians have the Holy Spirit?

Acts 2:38
Then Peter said unto them, Repent, and be baptized every one of you in the name of Jesus Christ for the remission of sins, and ye shall receive the gift of the Holy Ghost.

John 7:38-39
He that believeth on me, as the scripture hath said, out of his belly shall flow rivers of living water. (But this spake he of the Spirit, which they that believe on him should receive: for the Holy Ghost was not yet given; because that Jesus was not yet glorified.)

1 Corinthians 6:19
What? know ye not that your body is the temple of the Holy Ghost which is in you, which ye have of God, and ye are not your own?

Romans 8:16
The Spirit itself beareth witness with our spirit, that we are the children of God.

1 John 4:13
Hereby know we that we dwell in him, and he in us, because he hath given us of his Spirit.

Romans 8:9

But ye are not in the flesh, but in the Spirit, if so be that the Spirit of God dwell in you. Now if any man have not the Spirit of Christ, he is none of his.

1 Corinthians 2:14

But the natural man receiveth not the things of the Spirit of God: for they are foolishness unto him: neither can he know them, because they are spiritually discerned.

Romans 8:14

For as many as are led by the Spirit of God, they are the sons of God.

Ephesians 1:13-14

In whom ye also trusted, after that ye heard the word of truth, the gospel of your salvation: in whom also after that ye believed, ye were sealed with that holy Spirit of promise, Which is the earnest of our inheritance until the redemption of the purchased possession, unto the praise of his glory.

How can I be filled by the Holy Spirit?

Luke 11:13

If ye then, being evil, know how to give good gifts unto your children: how much more shall your heavenly Father give the Holy Spirit to them that ask him?

Hebrews 3:7-9

Wherefore as the Holy Ghost saith, To day if ye will hear his voice, Harden not your hearts, as in the provocation, in the day of temptation in the wilderness: When your fathers tempted me, proved me, and saw my works forty years.

Ephesians 5:18

And be not drunk with wine, wherein is excess; but be filled with the Spirit.

Matthew 12:31

Wherefore I say unto you, All manner of sin and blasphemy shall be forgiven unto men: but the blasphemy against the Holy Ghost shall not be forgiven unto men.

Matthew 7:7-8

Ask, and it shall be given you; seek, and ye shall find; knock, and it shall be opened unto you: For every one that asketh receiveth; and he that seeketh findeth; and to him that knocketh it shall be opened.

James 1:5

If any of you lack wisdom, let him ask of God, that giveth to all men liberally, and upbraideth not; and it shall be given him.

HOPE

Who is the source of hope?

Psalm 71:5

For thou art my hope, O Lord God: thou art my trust from my youth.

2 Thessalonians 2:16-17

Now our Lord Jesus Christ himself, and God, even our Father, which hath loved us, and hath given us everlasting consolation and good hope through grace, Comfort your hearts, and stablish you in every good word and work.

Hebrews 11:1

Now faith is the substance of things hoped for, the evidence of things not seen.

Romans 5:1-2

Therefore being justified by faith, we have peace with God through our Lord Jesus Christ: By whom also we have access by faith into this grace wherein we stand, and rejoice in hope of the glory of God.

1 Thessalonians 1:2-3

We give thanks to God always for you all, making mention of you in our prayers; Remembering without ceasing your work of faith, and labour of love, and patience of hope in our Lord Jesus Christ, in the sight of God and our Father.

How can I have hope today?

Psalm 42:11

Why art thou cast down, O my soul? and why art thou disquieted within me? hope thou in God: for I shall yet praise him, who is the health of my countenance, and my God.

Romans 15:13

Now the God of hope fill you with all joy and peace in believing, that ye may abound in hope, through the power of the Holy Ghost.

Psalm 119:43

And take not the word of truth utterly out of my mouth; for I have hoped in thy judgments.

Colossians 1:23

If ye continue in the faith grounded and settled, and be not moved away from the hope of the gospel, which ye have heard, and which was preached to every creature which is under heaven; whereof I Paul am made a minister.

What is my hope for the future?

Titus 2:13-14

Looking for that blessed hope, and the glorious appearing of the great God and our Saviour Jesus Christ; Who gave himself for us, that he might redeem us from all iniquity, and purify unto himself a peculiar people, zealous of good works.

Colossians 1:27

To whom God would make known what is the riches of the glory of this mystery among the Gentiles; which is Christ in you, the hope of glory.

1 Thessalonians 4:16-18

For the Lord himself shall descend from heaven with a shout, with the voice of the archangel, and with the trump of God: and the dead in Christ shall rise first: Then we which are alive and remain shall be caught up together with them in the clouds, to meet the Lord in the air: and so shall we ever be with the Lord. Wherefore comfort one another with these words.

Colossians 1:3-5

We give thanks to God and the Father of our Lord Jesus Christ, praying always for you, Since we heard of your faith in Christ Jesus, and of the love which ye have to all the saints, For the hope which is laid up for you in heaven, whereof ye heard before in the word of the truth of the gospel.

Romans 8:22-25

For we know that the whole creation groaneth and travaileth in pain together until now. And not only they, but ourselves also, which have the firstfruits of the Spirit, even we ourselves groan within ourselves, waiting for the adoption, to wit, the redemption of our body. For we are saved by hope: but hope that is seen is not hope: for what a man seeth, why doth he yet hope for? But if we hope for that we see not, then do we with patience wait for it.

HUMILITY

Why should I be humble?

James 4:10
Humble yourselves in the sight of the Lord, and he shall lift you up.

1 Peter 5:5-6
. . . Yea, all of you be subject one to another, and be clothed with humility: for God resisteth the proud, and giveth grace to the humble. Humble yourselves therefore under the mighty hand of God, that he may exalt you in due time.

2 Chronicles 7:14
If my people, which are called by my name, shall humble themselves, and pray, and seek my face, and turn from their wicked ways; then will I hear from heaven, and will forgive their sin, and will heal their land.

Psalm 10:17
Lord, thou hast heard the desire of the humble: thou wilt prepare their heart, thou wilt cause thine ear to hear.

Isaiah 57:15
For thus saith the high and lofty One that inhabiteth eternity, whose name is Holy; I dwell in the high and holy place, with him also that is of a contrite and hum-

ble spirit, to revive the spirit of the humble, and to revive the heart of the contrite ones.

Romans 12:3

For I say, through the grace given unto me, to every man that is among you, not to think of himself more highly than he ought to think; but to think soberly, according as God hath dealt to every man the measure of faith.

Isaiah 66:2

For all those things hath mine hand made, and all those things have been, saith the Lord: but to this man will I look, even to him that is poor and of a contrite spirit, and trembleth at my word.

Proverbs 15:33

The fear of the Lord is the instruction of wisdom; and before honour is humility.

Proverbs 22:4

By humility and the fear of the Lord are riches, and honour, and life.

Luke 14:7-11

And he put forth a parable to those which were bidden, when he marked how they chose out the chief rooms; saying unto them, When thou art bidden of any man to a wedding, sit not down in the highest room; lest a more honourable man than thou be bidden of him; And he that bade thee and him come and say to thee, Give this man place; and thou begin with shame to take the lowest room. But when thou art bidden, go and sit down in the lowest room; that when he that bade thee cometh, he may say unto thee, Friend, go up higher: then shalt thou have worship in the presence of them that sit at meat with thee. For whosoever exalteth himself shall be abased; and he that humbleth himself shall be exalted.

What will happen if I'm not humble?

Psalm 18:27
For thou wilt save the afflicted people; but wilt bring down high looks.

Matthew 23:12
And whosoever shall exalt himself shall be abased; and he that shall humble himself shall be exalted.

Luke 1:52
He hath put down the mighty from their seats, and exalted them of low degree.

1 Samuel 2:3-5
Talk no more so exceeding proudly; let not arrogancy come out of your mouth: for the Lord is a God of knowledge, and by him actions are weighed. The bows of the mighty men are broken, and they that stumbled are girded with strength. They that were full have hired out themselves for bread; and they that were hungry ceased: so that the barren hath born seven; and she that hath many children is waxed feeble.

Psalm 12:3-4
The Lord shall cut off all flattering lips, and the tongue that speaketh proud things: Who have said, With our tongue will we prevail; our lips are our own: who is lord over us?

Jeremiah 50:31-32

Behold, I am against thee, O thou most proud, saith the Lord God of hosts: for thy day is come, the time that I will visit thee. And the most proud shall stumble and fall, and none shall raise him up: and I will kindle a fire in his cities, and it shall devour all round about him.

Who can I look to for an example of humility?

Philippians 2:3-8

Let nothing be done through strife or vainglory; but in lowliness of mind let each esteem other better than themselves. Look not every man on his own things, but every man also on the things of others. Let this mind be in you, which was also in Christ Jesus: Who, being in the form of God, thought it not robbery to be equal with God: But made himself of no reputation, and took upon him the form of a servant, and was made in the likeness of men: And being found in fashion as a man, he humbled himself, and became obedient unto death, even the death of the cross.

Matthew 8:5-10

And when Jesus was entered into Capernaum, there came unto him a centurion, beseeching him, And saying, Lord, my servant lieth at home sick of the palsy, grievously tormented. And Jesus saith unto him, I will come and heal him. The centurion answered and said, Lord, I am not worthy that thou shouldest come under my roof: but speak the word only, and my servant shall be healed. For I am a man under authority, having soldiers under me: and I say to this man, Go, and he goeth; and to another, Come, and he cometh; and to my servant, Do this, and he doeth it. When Jesus heard it, he marvelled, and said to them that followed, Verily I say unto you, I have not found so great faith, no, not in Israel.

Luke 18:13-14

And the publican, standing afar off, would not lift up so much as his eyes unto heaven, but smote upon his breast, saying, God be merciful to me a sinner. I tell you, this man went down to his house justified rather than the other: for every one that exalteth himself shall be abased; and he that humbleth himself shall be exalted.

Numbers 12:1-9

And Miriam and Aaron spake against Moses because of the Ethiopian woman whom he had married: for he had married an Ethiopian woman. And they said, Hath the Lord indeed spoken only by Moses? hath he not spoken also by us? And the Lord heard it. (Now the man Moses was very meek, above all the men which were upon the face of the earth.) And the Lord spake suddenly unto Moses, and unto Aaron, and unto Miriam, Come out ye three unto the tabernacle of the congregation. And they three came out. And the Lord came down in the pillar of the cloud, and stood in the door of the tabernacle, and called Aaron and Miriam: and they both came forth. And he said, Hear now my words: If there be a prophet among you, I the Lord will make myself known unto him in a vision, and will speak unto him in a dream. My servant Moses is not so, who is faithful in all mine house. With him will I speak mouth to mouth, even apparently, and not in dark speeches; and the similitude of the Lord shall he behold: wherefore then were ye not afraid to speak against my servant Moses? And the anger of the Lord was kindled against them; and he departed.

JOY

What is true joy?

Psalm 16:11
Thou wilt shew me the path of life: in thy presence is fulness of joy; at thy right hand there are pleasures for evermore.

Psalm 30:5
For his anger endureth but a moment; in his favour is life: weeping may endure for a night, but joy cometh in the morning.

Psalm 21:1
The king shall joy in thy strength, O Lord; and in thy salvation how greatly shall he rejoice!

John 16:33
These things I have spoken unto you, that in me ye might have peace. In the world ye shall have tribulation: but be of good cheer; I have overcome the world.

Nehemiah 8:10
Then he said unto them, Go your way, eat the fat, and drink the sweet, and send portions unto them for whom nothing is prepared: for this day is holy unto our Lord: neither be ye sorry; for the joy of the Lord is your strength.

Psalm 126:5
They that sow in tears shall reap in joy.

Luke 10:19-20
Behold, I give unto you power to tread on serpents and scorpions, and over all the power of the enemy: and nothing shall by any means hurt you. Notwithstanding in this rejoice not, that the spirits are subject unto you; but rather rejoice, because your names are written in heaven.

John 16:22-24
And ye now therefore have sorrow: but I will see you again, and your heart shall rejoice, and your joy no man taketh from you. And in that day ye shall ask me nothing. Verily, verily, I say unto you, Whatsoever ye shall ask the Father in my name, he will give it you. Hitherto have ye asked nothing in my name: ask, and ye shall receive, that your joy may be full.

What is the source of joy?

Psalm 4:7

Thou hast put gladness in my heart, more than in the time that their corn and their wine increased.

Galatians 5:22

But the fruit of the Spirit is love, joy, peace, longsuffering, gentleness, goodness, faith.

Isaiah 61:3

To appoint unto them that mourn in Zion, to give unto them beauty for ashes, the oil of joy for mourning, the garment of praise for the spirit of heaviness; that they might be called trees of righteousness, the planting of the Lord, that he might be glorified.

Jeremiah 15:16

Thy words were found, and I did eat them; and thy word was unto me the joy and rejoicing of mine heart: for I am called by thy name, O Lord God of hosts.

Psalm 16:11

Thou wilt shew me the path of life: in thy presence is fulness of joy; at thy right hand there are pleasures for evermore.

Isaiah 61:10
I will greatly rejoice in the Lord, my soul shall be joyful in my God; for he hath clothed me with the garments of salvation, he hath covered me with the robe of righteousness, as a bridegroom decketh himself with ornaments, and as a bride adorneth herself with her jewels.

Luke 15:10
Likewise, I say unto you, there is joy in the presence of the angels of God over one sinner that repenteth.

To whom does God promise joy?

1 Peter 1:8
Whom having not seen, ye love; in whom, though now ye see him not, yet believing, ye rejoice with joy unspeakable and full of glory.

Psalm 97:11
Light is sown for the righteous, and gladness for the upright in heart.

Psalm 132:9
Let thy priests be clothed with righteousness; and let thy saints shout for joy.

Proverbs 12:20
Deceit is in the heart of them that imagine evil: but to the counsellors of peace is joy.

Proverbs 21:15
It is joy to the just to do judgment: but destruction shall be to the workers of iniquity.

Proverbs 15:23
A man hath joy by the answer of his mouth: and a word spoken in due season, how good is it!

How can I be filled with joy?

Psalm 118:24
This is the day which the Lord hath made; we will rejoice and be glad in it.

Philippians 4:4
Rejoice in the Lord alway: and again I say, Rejoice.

Philippians 4:6
Be careful for nothing; but in every thing by prayer and supplication with thanksgiving let your requests be made known unto God.

Psalm 51:12
Restore unto me the joy of thy salvation; and uphold me with thy free spirit.

Psalm 119:162
I rejoice at thy word, as one that findeth great spoil.

Psalm 100:2
Serve the Lord with gladness: come before his presence with singing.

Matthew 25:21
His lord said unto him, Well done, thou good and faithful servant: thou hast been faithful over a few

things, I will make thee ruler over many things: enter thou into the joy of thy lord.

Luke 6:22-23

Blessed are ye, when men shall hate you, and when they shall separate you from their company, and shall reproach you, and cast out your name as evil, for the Son of man's sake. Rejoice ye in that day, and leap for joy: for, behold, your reward is great in heaven: for in the like manner did their fathers unto the prophets.

How should I express my joy?

Luke 19:37

And when he was come nigh, even now at the descent of the mount of Olives, the whole multitude of the disciples began to rejoice and praise God with a loud voice for all the mighty works that they had seen.

Psalm 2:11

Serve the Lord with fear, and rejoice with trembling.

2 Corinthians 6:10

As sorrowful, yet alway rejoicing; as poor, yet making many rich; as having nothing, and yet possessing all things.

Psalm 32:11

Be glad in the Lord, and rejoice, ye righteous: and shout for joy, all ye that are upright in heart.

Proverbs 15:13

A merry heart maketh a cheerful countenance: but by sorrow of the heart the spirit is broken.

James 5:13

Is any among you afflicted? let him pray. Is any merry? let him sing psalms.

Proverbs 17:22
A merry heart doeth good like a medicine: but a broken spirit drieth the bones.

Psalm 100:1-2
Make a joyful noise unto the Lord, all ye lands. Serve the Lord with gladness: come before his presence with singing.

Psalm 150:6
Let every thing that hath breath praise the Lord. Praise ye the Lord.

When should I rejoice?

Philippians 4:4
Rejoice in the Lord alway: and again I say, Rejoice.

Habakkuk 3:17
Although the fig tree shall not blossom, neither shall fruit be in the vines; the labour of the olive shall fail, and the fields shall yield no meat; the flock shall be cut off from the fold, and there shall be no herd in the stalls. Yet I will rejoice in the LORD, I will joy in the God of my salvation.

Hebrews 10:34
For ye had compassion of me in my bonds, and took joyfully the spoiling of your goods, knowing in yourselves that ye have in heaven a better and an enduring substance.

1 Peter 4:12-13
Beloved, think it not strange concerning the fiery trial which is to try you, as though some strange thing happened unto you: But rejoice, inasmuch as ye are partakers of Christ's sufferings; that, when his glory shall be revealed, ye may be glad also with exceeding joy.

Romans 12:15
Rejoice with them that do rejoice, and weep with them that weep.

Philippians 1:3-4
I thank my God upon every remembrance of you, Always in every prayer of mine for you all making request with joy.

Philippians 2:1-2
If there be therefore any consolation in Christ, if any comfort of love, if any fellowship of the Spirit, if any bowels and mercies, Fulfil ye my joy, that ye be likeminded, having the same love, being of one accord, of one mind,

LONELINESS

How did God's people respond to loneliness?

Psalm 142:4-5
I looked on my right hand, and beheld, but there was no man that would know me: refuge failed me; no man cared for my soul. I cried unto thee, O Lord: I said, Thou art my refuge and my portion in the land of the living.

John 16:32
Behold, the hour cometh, yea, is now come, that ye shall be scattered, every man to his own, and shall leave me alone: and yet I am not alone, because the Father is with me.

Luke 15:18-20
I will arise and go to my father, and will say unto him, Father, I have sinned against heaven, and before thee, And am no more worthy to be called thy son: make me as one of thy hired servants. And he arose, and came to his father. But when he was yet a great way off, his father saw him, and had compassion, and ran, and fell on his neck, and kissed him.

2 Timothy 4:16
At my first answer no man stood with me, but all men forsook me: I pray God that it may not be laid to their charge.

Jeremiah 15:17
I sat not in the assembly of the mockers, nor rejoiced; I sat alone because of thy hand: for thou hast filled me with indignation.

Jeremiah 15:19
Therefore thus saith the Lord, If thou return, then will I bring thee again, and thou shalt stand before me: and if thou take forth the precious from the vile, thou shalt be as my mouth: let them return unto thee; but return not thou unto them.

Ezekiel 9:8
And it came to pass, while they were slaying them, and I was left, that I fell upon my face, and cried, and said, Ah Lord God! wilt thou destroy all the residue of Israel in thy pouring out of thy fury upon Jerusalem?

Why am I lonely?

1 Peter 2:11
Dearly beloved, I beseech you as strangers and pilgrims, abstain from fleshly lusts, which war against the soul.

John 15:19
If ye were of the world, the world would love his own: but because ye are not of the world, but I have chosen you out of the world, therefore the world hateth you.

Psalm 142:4
I looked on my right hand, and beheld, but there was no man that would know me: refuge failed me; no man cared for my soul.

Psalm 88:18
Lover and friend hast thou put far from me, and mine acquaintance into darkness.

Psalm 38:11
My lovers and my friends stand aloof from my sore; and my kinsmen stand afar off.

Proverbs 27:8
As a bird that wandereth from her nest, so is a man that wandereth from his place.

Matthew 10:22
And ye shall be hated of all men for my name's sake: but he that endureth to the end shall be saved.

Does God care if I am lonely?

Psalm 4:8
I will both lay me down in peace, and sleep: for thou, Lord, only makest me dwell in safety.

Psalm 68:5-6
A father of the fatherless, and a judge of the widows, is God in his holy habitation. God setteth the solitary in families: he bringeth out those which are bound with chains: but the rebellious dwell in a dry land.

Joshua 1:5
There shall not any man be able to stand before thee all the days of thy life: as I was with Moses, so I will be with thee: I will not fail thee, nor forsake thee.

Isaiah 54:10
For the mountains shall depart, and the hills be removed; but my kindness shall not depart from thee, neither shall the covenant of my peace be removed, saith the Lord that hath mercy on thee.

John 14:18
I will not leave you comfortless: I will come to you.

2 Timothy 4:17
Notwithstanding the Lord stood with me, and

strengthened me; that by me the preaching might be fully known, and that all the Gentiles might hear: and I was delivered out of the mouth of the lion.

John 15:15

Henceforth I call you not servants; for the servant knoweth not what his lord doeth: but I have called you friends; for all things that I have heard of my Father I have made known unto you.

Psalm 38:9

Lord, all my desire is before thee; and my groaning is not hid from thee.

Psalm 34:18

The Lord is nigh unto them that are of a broken heart; and saveth such as be of a contrite spirit.

What should I do when I feel lonely?

Psalm 38:15
For in thee, O Lord, do I hope: thou wilt hear, O Lord my God.

Micah 7:5
Trust ye not in a friend, put ye not confidence in a guide: keep the doors of thy mouth from her that lieth in thy bosom.

1 John 1:7
But if we walk in the light, as he is in the light, we have fellowship one with another, and the blood of Jesus Christ his Son cleanseth us from all sin.

Colossians 3:15
And let the peace of God rule in your hearts, to the which also ye are called in one body; and be ye thankful.

2 Corinthians 1:3-4
Blessed be God, even the Father of our Lord Jesus Christ, the Father of mercies, and the God of all comfort; Who comforteth us in all our tribulation, that we may be able to comfort them which are in any trouble, by the comfort wherewith we ourselves are comforted of God.

Ecclesiastes 4:9-10

Two are better than one; because they have a good reward for their labour. For if they fall, the one will lift up his fellow: but woe to him that is alone when he falleth; for he hath not another to help him up.

Psalm 73:23-26

Nevertheless I am continually with thee: thou hast holden me by my right hand. Thou shalt guide me with thy counsel, and afterward receive me to glory. Whom have I in heaven but thee? and there is none upon earth that I desire beside thee. My flesh and my heart faileth: but God is the strength of my heart, and my portion for ever.

What should I do when I feel far away from God?

Psalm 22:1
My God, my God, why hast thou forsaken me? why art thou so far from helping me, and from the words of my roaring?

1 Peter 2:25
For ye were as sheep going astray; but are now returned unto the Shepherd and Bishop of your souls.

Psalm 61:2
From the end of the earth will I cry unto thee, when my heart is overwhelmed: lead me to the rock that is higher than I.

Psalm 84:5, 7
Blessed is the man whose strength is in thee; in whose heart are the ways of them.
They go from strength to strength, every one of them in Zion appeareth before God.

Acts 17:26-28
[God] hath determined the times before appointed, and the bounds of their habitation; That they should seek the Lord, if haply they might feel after him, and find him, though he be not far from every one of us:

For in him we live, and move, and have our being; as certain also of your own poets have said, For we are also his offspring.

Hebrews 10:22
Let us draw near with a true heart in full assurance of faith, having our hearts sprinkled from an evil conscience, and our bodies washed with pure water.

LOVE

What is God's love like?

Ephesians 3:16-19

That he would grant you, according to the riches of his glory, to be strengthened with might by his Spirit in the inner man; That Christ may dwell in your hearts by faith; that ye, being rooted and grounded in love, May be able to comprehend with all saints what is the breadth, and length, and depth, and height; And to know the love of Christ, which passeth knowledge, that ye might be filled with all the fulness of God.

1 Corinthians 13:4-8, 13

Charity suffereth long, and is kind; charity envieth not; charity vaunteth not itself, is not puffed up, Doth not behave itself unseemly, seeketh not her own, is not easily provoked, thinketh no evil; Rejoiceth not in iniquity, but rejoiceth in the truth; Beareth all things, believeth all things, hopeth all things, endureth all things. Charity never faileth: but whether there be prophecies, they shall fail; whether there be tongues, they shall cease; whether there be knowledge, it shall vanish away. And now abideth faith, hope, charity, these three; but the greatest of these is charity.

1 John 4:17-18

Herein is our love made perfect, that we may have boldness in the day of judgment: because as he is, so are we in this world. There is no fear in love; but perfect love casteth out fear: because fear hath torment. He that feareth is not made perfect in love.

Romans 8:38-39

For I am persuaded, that neither death, nor life, nor angels, nor principalities, nor powers, nor things present, nor things to come, Nor height, nor depth, nor any other creature, shall be able to separate us from the love of God, which is in Christ Jesus our Lord.

Does God love me?

John 3:16

For God so loved the world, that he gave his only begotten Son, that whosoever believeth in him should not perish, but have everlasting life.

Jeremiah 31:3

The Lord hath appeared of old unto me, saying, Yea, I have loved thee with an everlasting love: therefore with lovingkindness have I drawn thee.

1 John 4:15-16

Whosoever shall confess that Jesus is the Son of God, God dwelleth in him, and he in God. And we have known and believed the love that God hath to us. God is love; and he that dwelleth in love dwelleth in God, and God in him.

How has God demonstrated his love?

1 John 4:9-10

In this was manifested the love of God toward us, because that God sent his only begotten Son into the world, that we might live through him. Herein is love, not that we loved God, but that he loved us, and sent his Son to be the propitiation for our sins.

Romans 5:7-9

For scarcely for a righteous man will one die: yet peradventure for a good man some would even dare to die. But God commendeth his love toward us, in that, while we were yet sinners, Christ died for us. Much more then, being now justified by his blood, we shall be saved from wrath through him.

1 John 3:1

Behold, what manner of love the Father hath bestowed upon us, that we should be called the sons of God: therefore the world knoweth us not, because it knew him not.

John 15:13-16

Greater love hath no man than this, that a man lay down his life for his friends. Ye are my friends, if ye do whatsoever I command you. Henceforth I call you not servants; for the servant knoweth not what his lord doeth: but I have called you friends; for all things that I have heard of my Father I have made known unto you. Ye have not chosen me, but I have chosen you, and ordained you, that ye should go and bring forth fruit, and that your fruit should remain: that whatsoever ye shall ask of the Father in my name, he may give it you.

How do I show that I love God?

1 John 5:3

For this is the love of God, that we keep his commandments: and his commandments are not grievous.

1 John 4:19-21

We love him, because he first loved us. If a man say, I love God, and hateth his brother, he is a liar: for he that loveth not his brother whom he hath seen, how can he love God whom he hath not seen? And this commandment have we from him, That he who loveth God love his brother also.

1 John 3:10-12

In this the children of God are manifest, and the children of the devil: whosoever doeth not righteousness is not of God, neither he that loveth not his brother. For this is the message that ye heard from the beginning, that we should love one another. Not as Cain, who was of that wicked one, and slew his brother. And wherefore slew he him? Because his own works were evil, and his brother's righteous.

John 15:9-10

As the Father hath loved me, so have I loved you: continue ye in my love. If ye keep my commandments, ye shall abide in my love; even as I have kept my Father's commandments, and abide in his love.

1 John 2:9-11

He that saith he is in the light, and hateth his brother, is in darkness even until now. He that loveth his brother abideth in the light, and there is none occasion of stumbling in him. But he that hateth his brother is in darkness, and walketh in darkness, and knoweth not whither he goeth, because that darkness hath blinded his eyes.

1 John 3:23-24

And this is his commandment, That we should believe on the name of his Son Jesus Christ, and love one another, as he gave us commandment. And he that keepeth his commandments dwelleth in him, and he in him. And hereby we know that he abideth in us, by the Spirit which he hath given us.

Why should I love others?

John 15:12

This is my commandment, That ye love one another, as I have loved you.

Mark 12:28-31

And one of the scribes came, and having heard them reasoning together, and perceiving that he had answered them well, asked him, Which is the first commandment of all? And Jesus answered him, The first of all the commandments is, Hear, O Israel; The Lord our God is one Lord: And thou shalt love the Lord thy God with all thy heart, and with all thy soul, and with all thy mind, and with all thy strength: this is the first commandment. And the second is like, namely this, Thou shalt love thy neighbour as thyself. There is none other commandment greater than these.

1 John 3:16

Hereby perceive we the love of God, because he laid down his life for us: and we ought to lay down our lives for the brethren.

1 John 4:7-8

Beloved, let us love one another: for love is of God; and every one that loveth is born of God, and knoweth God. He that loveth not knoweth not God; for God is love.

1 John 4:11-12

Beloved, if God so loved us, we ought also to love one another. No man hath seen God at any time. If we love one another, God dwelleth in us, and his love is perfected in us.

1 Peter 4:8

And above all things have fervent charity among yourselves: for charity shall cover the multitude of sins.

How should I love others?

1 Corinthians 16:14
Let all your things be done with charity.

1 John 3:17-18
But whoso hath this world's good, and seeth his brother have need, and shutteth up his bowels of compassion from him, how dwelleth the love of God in him? My little children, let us not love in word, neither in tongue; but in deed and in truth.

2 John 1:5-6
And now I beseech thee, lady, not as though I wrote a new commandment unto thee, but that which we had from the beginning, that we love one another. And this is love, that we walk after his commandments. This is the commandment, That, as ye have heard from the beginning, ye should walk in it.

Philippians 1:9-11
And this I pray, that your love may abound yet more and more in knowledge and in all judgment; That ye may approve things that are excellent; that ye may be sincere and without offence till the day of Christ; Being filled with the fruits of righteousness, which are by Jesus Christ, unto the glory and praise of God.

Ephesians 5:1-2
Be ye therefore followers of God, as dear children; And walk in love, as Christ also hath loved us, and hath given himself for us an offering and a sacrifice to God for a sweetsmelling savour.

Colossians 3:12-14
Put on therefore, as the elect of God, holy and beloved, bowels of mercies, kindness, humbleness of mind, meekness, longsuffering; Forbearing one another, and forgiving one another, if any man have a quarrel against any: even as Christ forgave you, so also do ye. And above all these things put on charity, which is the bond of perfectness.

MARRIAGE

Why is marriage special?

Genesis 2:22-24

And the rib, which the Lord God had taken from man, made he a woman, and brought her unto the man. And Adam said, This is now bone of my bones, and flesh of my flesh: she shall be called Woman, because she was taken out of Man. Therefore shall a man leave his father and his mother, and shall cleave unto his wife: and they shall be one flesh.

Ephesians 5:31-32

For this cause shall a man leave his father and mother, and shall be joined unto his wife, and they two shall be one flesh. This is a great mystery: but I speak concerning Christ and the church.

Proverbs 18:22

Whoso findeth a wife findeth a good thing, and obtaineth favour of the Lord.

Genesis 2:18

And the Lord God said, It is not good that the man should be alone; I will make him an help meet for him.

Proverbs 5:18-19

Let thy fountain be blessed: and rejoice with the wife of thy youth. Let her be as the loving hind and pleasant roe; let her breasts satisfy thee at all times; and be thou ravished always with her love.

What makes a godly marriage?

Genesis 2:24

Therefore shall a man leave his father and his mother, and shall cleave unto his wife: and they shall be one flesh.

1 Corinthians 7:10-11

And unto the married I command, yet not I, but the Lord, Let not the wife depart from her husband: But and if she depart, let her remain unmarried, or be reconciled to her husband: and let not the husband put away his wife.

Song of Songs 8:7

Many waters cannot quench love, neither can the floods drown it: if a man would give all the substance of his house for love, it would utterly be contemned.

1 Corinthians 7:2-4

Nevertheless, to avoid fornication, let every man have his own wife, and let every woman have her own husband. Let the husband render unto the wife due benevolence: and likewise also the wife unto the husband. The wife hath not power of her own body, but the husband: and likewise also the husband hath not power of his own body, but the wife.

Hebrews 13:4
Marriage is honourable in all, and the bed undefiled: but whoremongers and adulterers God will judge.

Joshua 24:15
Choose you this day whom ye will serve...but as for me and my house, we will serve the Lord.

2 Corinthians 6:14
Be ye not unequally yoked together with unbelievers: for what fellowship hath righteousness with unrighteousness? and what communion hath light with darkness?

How should I treat my marriage partner?

Matthew 19:6
Wherefore they are no more twain, but one flesh. What therefore God hath joined together, let not man put asunder.

Mark 10:9
What therefore God hath joined together, let not man put asunder.

1 Corinthians 7:3
Let the husband render unto the wife due benevolence: and likewise also the wife unto the husband.

1 Corinthians 7:4-5
The wife hath not power of her own body, but the husband: and likewise also the husband hath not power of his own body, but the wife. Defraud ye not one the other, except it be with consent for a time, that ye may give yourselves to fasting and prayer; and come together again, that Satan tempt you not for your incontinency.

Ephesians 5:33
Nevertheless let every one of you in particular so love his wife even as himself; and the wife see that she reverence her husband.

Romans 15:5-6
Now the God of patience and consolation grant you to be likeminded one toward another according to Christ Jesus: That ye may with one mind and one mouth glorify God, even the Father of our Lord Jesus Christ.

Ephesians 5:21
Submitting yourselves one to another in the fear of God.

James 5:16
Confess your faults one to another, and pray one for another, that ye may be healed.

Colossians 3:14
And above all these things put on charity, which is the bond of perfectness.

How can a man best love his wife?

Ephesians 5:23
For the husband is the head of the wife, even as Christ is the head of the church: and he is the saviour of the body.

Ephesians 5:25-26
Husbands, love your wives, even as Christ also loved the church, and gave himself for it; That he might sanctify and cleanse it with the washing of water by the word.

Ephesians 5:28-29
So ought men to love their wives as their own bodies. He that loveth his wife loveth himself. For no man ever yet hated his own flesh; but nourisheth and cherisheth it, even as the Lord the church.

1 Peter 3:7
Likewise, ye husbands, dwell with them according to knowledge, giving honour unto the wife, as unto the weaker vessel, and as being heirs together of the grace of life; that your prayers be not hindered.

Colossians 3:19
Husbands, love your wives, and be not bitter against them.

1 Corinthians 7:11
But and if she depart, let her remain unmarried, or be reconciled to her husband: and let not the husband put away his wife.

How can I be a good husband?

Colossians 3:19
Husbands, love your wives, and be not bitter against them.

Ecclesiastes 9:9
Live joyfully with the wife whom thou lovest all the days of the life of thy vanity, which he hath given thee under the sun, all the days of thy vanity: for that is thy portion in this life, and in thy labour which thou takest under the sun.

Proverbs 5:18
Let thy fountain be blessed: and rejoice with the wife of thy youth.

Proverbs 31:28-29
Her children arise up, and call her blessed; her husband also, and he praiseth her. Many daughters have done virtuously, but thou excellest them all.

Proverbs 5:15-17
Drink waters out of thine own cistern, and running waters out of thine own well. Let thy fountains be dispersed abroad, and rivers of waters in the streets. Let them be only thine own, and not strangers' with thee.

Malachi 2:15
And did not he make one? Yet had he the residue of the spirit. And wherefore one? That he might seek a godly seed. Therefore take heed to your spirit, and let none deal treacherously against the wife of his youth.

Ephesians 5:25-26
Husbands, love your wives, even as Christ also loved the church, and gave himself for it; That he might sanctify and cleanse it with the washing of water by the word.

Exodus 20:17
Thou shalt not covet thy neighbour's house, thou shalt not covet thy neighbour's wife, nor his manservant, nor his maidservant, nor his ox, nor his ass, nor any thing that is thy neighbour's.

How can a woman best love her husband?

Genesis 2:18
And the Lord God said, It is not good that the man should be alone; I will make him an help meet for him.

Titus 2:4
That they may teach the young women to be sober, to love their husbands, to love their children.

Ephesians 5:33
Nevertheless let every one of you in particular so love his wife even as himself; and the wife see that she reverence her husband.

1 Peter 3:1-2
Likewise, ye wives, be in subjection to your own husbands; that, if any obey not the word, they also may without the word be won by the conversation of the wives; While they behold your chaste conversation coupled with fear.

Titus 2:5
To be discreet, chaste, keepers at home, good, obedient to their own husbands, that the word of God be not blasphemed.

1 Corinthians 7:10
And unto the married I command, yet not I, but the Lord, Let not the wife depart from her husband.

How can I be a good wife?

Proverbs 31:30
Favour is deceitful, and beauty is vain: but a woman that feareth the Lord, she shall be praised.

Proverbs 12:4
A virtuous woman is a crown to her husband: but she that maketh ashamed is as rottenness in his bones.

Proverbs 31:11
The heart of her husband doth safely trust in her, so that he shall have no need of spoil.

Titus 2:5
To be discreet, chaste, keepers at home, good, obedient to their own husbands, that the word of God be not blasphemed.

Proverbs 31:13
She seeketh wool, and flax, and worketh willingly with her hands.

Proverbs 31:27
She looketh well to the ways of her household, and eateth not the bread of idleness.

Proverbs 19:14

House and riches are the inheritance of fathers and a prudent wife is from the Lord.

Proverbs 10:16

The labour of the righteous tendeth to life: the fruit of the wicked to sin.

MONEY

What does God teach me about money?

Proverbs 23:5
Wilt thou set thine eyes upon that which is not? for riches certainly make themselves wings; they fly away as an eagle toward heaven.

1 Timothy 6:7
For we brought nothing into this world, and it is certain we can carry nothing out.

Ecclesiastes 5:10
He that loveth silver shall not be satisfied with silver; nor he that loveth abundance with increase: this is also vanity.

Luke 12:15
And he said unto them, Take heed, and beware of covetousness: for a man's life consisteth not in the abundance of the things which he possesseth.

Hebrews 13:5
Let your conversation be without covetousness; and be content with such things as ye have: for he hath said, I will never leave thee, nor forsake thee.

Psalm 62:10
Trust not in oppression, and become not vain in robbery: if riches increase, set not your heart upon them.

1 Timothy 6:9

But they that will be rich fall into temptation and a snare, and into many foolish and hurtful lusts, which drown men in destruction and perdition.

Proverbs 11:28

He that trusteth in his riches shall fall: but the righteous shall flourish as a branch.

Does God reward goodness with wealth?

Ecclesiastes 5:19

Every man also to whom God hath given riches and wealth, and hath given him power to eat thereof, and to take his portion, and to rejoice in his labour; this is the gift of God.

Proverbs 28:20

A faithful man shall abound with blessings: but he that maketh haste to be rich shall not be innocent.

Proverbs 28:19

He that tilleth his land shall have plenty of bread: but he that followeth after vain persons shall have poverty enough.

1 Thessalonians 4:11-12

And that ye study to be quiet, and to do your own business, and to work with your own hands, as we commanded you; That ye may walk honestly toward them that are without, and that ye may have lack of nothing.

Luke 6:38

Give, and it shall be given unto you; good measure, pressed down, and shaken together, and running over, shall men give into your bosom. For with the same measure that ye mete withal it shall be measured to you again.

Does God cause poverty?

Job 34:19
How much less to him that accepteth not the persons of princes, nor regardeth the rich more than the poor? for they all are the work of his hands.

1 Samuel 2:8
He raiseth up the poor out of the dust, and lifteth up the beggar from the dunghill, to set them among princes, and to make them inherit the throne of glory: for the pillars of the earth are the Lord's, and he hath set the world upon them.

James 2:5
Hearken, my beloved brethren, Hath not God chosen the poor of this world rich in faith, and heirs of the kingdom which he hath promised to them that love him?

Proverbs 6:10-11
Yet a little sleep, a little slumber, a little folding of the hands to sleep: So shall thy poverty come as one that travelleth, and thy want as an armed man.

Proverbs 28:19
He that tilleth his land shall have plenty of bread: but he that followeth after vain persons shall have poverty enough.

What if I have very little money?

Matthew 6:31-33

Therefore take no thought, saying, What shall we eat? or, What shall we drink? or, Wherewithal shall we be clothed? (For after all these things do the Gentiles seek:) for your heavenly Father knoweth that ye have need of all these things. But seek ye first the kingdom of God, and his righteousness; and all these things shall be added unto you.

Psalm 102:17

He will regard the prayer of the destitute, and not despise their prayer.

Psalm 68:10

Thy congregation hath dwelt therein: thou, O God, hast prepared of thy goodness for the poor.

Proverbs 19:1

Better is the poor that walketh in his integrity, than he that is perverse in his lips, and is a fool.

1 Timothy 6:7-8

For we brought nothing into this world, and it is certain we can carry nothing out. And having food and raiment let us be therewith content.

Mark 12:43-44
And he called unto him his disciples, and saith unto them, Verily I say unto you, That this poor widow hath cast more in, than all they which have cast into the treasury: For all they did cast in of their abundance; but she of her want did cast in all that she had, even all her living.

How should I use my money?

Proverbs 3:9-10

Honour the Lord with thy substance, and with the firstfruits of all thine increase: So shall thy barns be filled with plenty, and thy presses shall burst out with new wine.

Malachi 3:10

Bring ye all the tithes into the storehouse, that there may be meat in mine house, and prove me now herewith, saith the Lord of hosts, if I will not open you the windows of heaven, and pour you out a blessing, that there shall not be room enough to receive it.

Hebrews 13:16

But to do good and to communicate forget not: for with such sacrifices God is well pleased.

Deuteronomy 15:10

Thou shalt surely give him, and thine heart shall not be grieved when thou givest unto him: because that for this thing the Lord thy God shall bless thee in all thy works, and in all that thou puttest thine hand unto.

Romans 13:8

Owe no man any thing, but to love one another: for he that loveth another hath fulfilled the law.

Proverbs 21:20
There is treasure to be desired and oil in the dwelling of the wise; but a foolish man spendeth it up.

Matthew 25:27
Thou oughtest therefore to have put my money to the exchangers, and then at my coming I should have received mine own with usury.

Matthew 6:19
Lay not up for yourselves treasures upon earth, where moth and rust doth corrupt, and where thieves break through and steal.

What are the dangers of money?

1 Timothy 6:10

For the love of money is the root of all evil: which while some coveted after, they have erred from the faith, and pierced themselves through with many sorrows.

Matthew 6:24

No man can serve two masters: for either he will hate the one, and love the other; or else he will hold to the one, and despise the other. Ye cannot serve God and mammon.

Matthew 19:23

Then said Jesus unto his disciples, Verily I say unto you, That a rich man shall hardly enter into the kingdom of heaven.

Mark 10:21-22

Then Jesus beholding him loved him, and said unto him, One thing thou lackest: go thy way, sell whatsoever thou hast, and give to the poor, and thou shalt have treasure in heaven: and come, take up the cross, and follow me. And he was sad at that saying, and went away grieved: for he had great possessions.

Mark 8:36

For what shall it profit a man, if he shall gain the whole world, and lose his own soul?

James 5:2-3

Your riches are corrupted, and your garments are motheaten. Your gold and silver is cankered; and the rust of them shall be a witness against you, and shall eat your flesh as it were fire. Ye have heaped treasure together for the last days.

Proverbs 22:7

The rich ruleth over the poor, and the borrower is servant to the lender.

Proverbs 6:1-3

My son, if thou be surety for thy friend, if thou hast stricken thy hand with a stranger, Thou art snared with the words of thy mouth, thou art taken with the words of thy mouth. Do this now, my son, deliver thyself, when thou art come into the hand of thy friend; go, humble thyself, and make sure thy friend.

[illegible]

[illegible]

[illegible]

[illegible]

[illegible]

PATIENCE

What is patience?

Hebrews 10:35-37

Cast not away therefore your confidence, which hath great recompence of reward. For ye have need of patience, that, after ye have done the will of God, ye might receive the promise. For yet a little while, and he that shall come will come, and will not tarry.

Ecclesiastes 7:8-9

Better is the end of a thing than the beginning thereof: and the patient in spirit is better than the proud in spirit. Be not hasty in thy spirit to be angry: for anger resteth in the bosom of fools.

1 Corinthians 13:4

Charity suffereth long, and is kind; charity envieth not; charity vaunteth not itself, is not puffed up.

Galatians 5:22

But the fruit of the Spirit is love, joy, peace, longsuffering, gentleness, goodness, faith.

Romans 8:25

But if we hope for that we see not, then do we with patience wait for it.

Psalm 37:7

Rest in the Lord, and wait patiently for him: fret not thyself because of him who prospereth in his way, because of the man who bringeth wicked devices to pass.

James 5:7-8

Be patient therefore, brethren, unto the coming of the Lord. Behold, the husbandman waiteth for the precious fruit of the earth, and hath long patience for it, until he receive the early and latter rain. Be ye also patient; stablish your hearts: for the coming of the Lord draweth nigh.

Ephesians 4:2

With all lowliness and meekness, with longsuffering, forbearing one another in love.

What are the benefits of patience?

Lamentations 3:25
The Lord is good unto them that wait for him, to the soul that seeketh him.

Psalm 40:1
I waited patiently for the Lord; and he inclined unto me, and heard my cry.

Isaiah 40:31
But they that wait upon the Lord shall renew their strength; they shall mount up with wings as eagles; they shall run, and not be weary; and they shall walk, and not faint.

Habakkuk 2:3
For the vision is yet for an appointed time, but at the end it shall speak, and not lie: though it tarry, wait for it; because it will surely come, it will not tarry.

Hebrews 6:12
That ye be not slothful, but followers of them who through faith and patience inherit the promises.

Luke 21:19
In your patience possess ye your souls.

Is God patient?

2 Peter 3:9

The Lord is not slack concerning his promise, as some men count slackness; but is longsuffering to us-ward, not willing that any should perish, but that all should come to repentance.

1 Timothy 1:16

Howbeit for this cause I obtained mercy, that in me first Jesus Christ might shew forth all longsuffering, for a pattern to them which should hereafter believe on him to life everlasting.

Romans 2:4

Or despisest thou the riches of his goodness and forbearance and longsuffering; not knowing that the goodness of God leadeth thee to repentance?

1 Peter 3:20

Which sometime were disobedient, when once the longsuffering of God waited in the days of Noah, while the ark was a preparing, wherein few, that is, eight souls were saved by water.

Numbers 14:18

The Lord is longsuffering, and of great mercy, forgiving iniquity and transgression, and by no means clearing the guilty, visiting the iniquity of the fathers upon the children unto the third and fourth generation.

Psalm 103:8
The Lord is merciful and gracious, slow to anger, and plenteous in mercy.

PEACE

How can I have peace in the midst of trials?

John 16:33

These things I have spoken unto you, that in me ye might have peace. In the world ye shall have tribulation: but be of good cheer; I have overcome the world.

Matthew 11:28-29

Come unto me, all ye that labour and are heavy laden, and I will give you rest. Take my yoke upon you, and learn of me; for I am meek and lowly in heart: and ye shall find rest unto your souls.

John 7:38

He that believeth on me, as the scripture hath said, out of his belly shall flow rivers of living water.

Is peace a choice?

1 Corinthians 7:15

But if the unbelieving depart, let him depart. A brother or a sister is not under bondage in such cases: but God hath called us to peace.

Colossians 3:15

And let the peace of God rule in your hearts, to the which also ye are called in one body; and be ye thankful.

PERSEVERANCE

What makes our faith persevere?

John 10:27-30

My sheep hear my voice, and I know them, and they follow me: And I give unto them eternal life; and they shall never perish, neither shall any man pluck them out of my hand. My Father, which gave them me, is greater than all; and no man is able to pluck them out of my Father's hand. I and my Father are one.

1 Peter 1:3-5

Blessed be the God and Father of our Lord Jesus Christ, which according to his abundant mercy hath begotten us again unto a lively hope by the resurrection of Jesus Christ from the dead, To an inheritance incorruptible, and undefiled, and that fadeth not away, reserved in heaven for you, Who are kept by the power of God through faith unto salvation ready to be revealed in the last time.

Matthew 10:22

And ye shall be hated of all men for my name's sake: but he that endureth to the end shall be saved.

1 Timothy 4:15-16

Meditate upon these things; give thyself wholly to them; that thy profiting may appear to all. Take heed unto thyself, and unto the doctrine; continue in them:

for in doing this thou shalt both save thyself, and them that hear thee.

James 1:12
Blessed is the man that endureth temptation: for when he is tried, he shall receive the crown of life, which the Lord hath promised to them that love him.

Why should I persevere in doing what is right?

Galatians 6:8-10
For he that soweth to his flesh shall of the flesh reap corruption; but he that soweth to the Spirit shall of the Spirit reap life everlasting. And let us not be weary in well doing: for in due season we shall reap, if we faint not. As we have therefore opportunity, let us do good unto all men, especially unto them who are of the household of faith.

James 1:2-4
My brethren, count it all joy when ye fall into divers temptations; Knowing this, that the trying of your faith worketh patience. But let patience have her perfect work, that ye may be perfect and entire, wanting nothing.

2 Peter 1:5-9
And beside this, giving all diligence, add to your faith virtue; and to virtue knowledge; And to knowledge temperance; and to temperance patience; and to patience godliness; And to godliness brotherly kindness; and to brotherly kindness charity. For if these things be in you, and abound, they make you that ye shall neither be barren nor unfruitful in the knowledge of our Lord Jesus Christ. But he that lacketh these

things is blind, and cannot see afar off, and hath forgotten that he was purged from his old sins.

1 Corinthians 15:58

Therefore, my beloved brethren, be ye stedfast, unmovable, always abounding in the work of the Lord, forasmuch as ye know that your labour is not in vain in the Lord.

2 Thessalonians 3:13

But ye, brethren, be not weary in well doing.

Romans 2:5-8

But after thy hardness and impenitent heart treasurest up unto thyself wrath against the day of wrath and revelation of the righteous judgment of God; Who will render to every man according to his deeds: To them who by patient continuance in well doing seek for glory and honour and immortality, eternal life: But unto them that are contentious, and do not obey the truth, but obey unrighteousness, indignation and wrath.

How should I perservere?

Hebrews 12:1-3

Wherefore seeing we also are compassed about with so great a cloud of witnesses, let us lay aside every weight, and the sin which doth so easily beset us, and let us run with patience the race that is set before us, Looking unto Jesus the author and finisher of our faith; who for the joy that was set before him endured the cross, despising the shame, and is set down at the right hand of the throne of God. For consider him that endured such contradiction of sinners against himself, lest ye be wearied and faint in your minds.

Ephesians 6:18

Praying always with all prayer and supplication in the Spirit, and watching thereunto with all perseverance and supplication for all saints.

1 Corinthians 13:7

[Charity] Beareth all things, believeth all things, hopeth all things, endureth all things.

Romans 5:3-5

And not only so, but we glory in tribulations also: knowing that tribulation worketh patience; And patience, experience; and experience, hope: And hope maketh not ashamed; because the love of God is shed abroad in our hearts by the Holy Ghost which is given unto us.

Philippians 3:12-14

Not as though I had already attained, either were already perfect: but I follow after, if that I may apprehend that for which also I am apprehended of Christ Jesus. Brethren, I count not myself to have apprehended: but this one thing I do, forgetting those things which are behind, and reaching forth unto those things which are before, I press toward the mark for the prize of the high calling of God in Christ Jesus.

PLEASURE

What can distract me from true pleasures?

Ecclesiastes 2:3

I sought in mine heart to give myself unto wine, yet acquainting mine heart with wisdom; and to lay hold on folly, till I might see what *was* that good for the sons of men, which they should do under the heaven all the days of their life.

Proverbs 21:17

He that loveth pleasure *shall be* a poor man: he that loveth wine and oil shall not be rich.

Ecclesiastes 2:2

I said of laughter, *It is* mad: and of mirth, What doeth it?

Luke 8:14

And that which fell among thorns are they, which, when they have heard, go forth, and are choked with cares and riches and pleasures of *this* life, and bring no fruit to perfection.

Ecclesiastes 2:11

Then I looked on all the works that my hands had wrought, and on the labour that I had laboured to do: and, behold, all *was* vanity and vexation of spirit, and *there was* no profit under the sun.

Galatians 5:19-21

Now the works of the flesh are manifest, which are *these;* Adultery, fornication, uncleanness, lasciviousness, Idolatry, witchcraft, hatred, variance, emulations, wrath, strife, seditions, heresies, Envyings, murders, drunkenness, revellings, and such like: of the which I tell you before, as I have also told *you* in time past, that they which do such things shall not inherit the kingdom of God.

What will truly please me?

Ecclesiastes 2:24

There is nothing better for a man, *than* that he should eat and drink, and *that* he should make his soul enjoy good in his labour. This also I saw, that it *was* from the hand of God.

Nehemiah 8:10

Then he said unto them, Go your way, eat the fat, and drink the sweet, and send portions unto them for whom nothing is prepared: for *this* day *is* holy unto our Lord: neither be ye sorry; for the joy of the LORD is your strength.

Isaiah 61:10

I will greatly rejoice in the LORD, my soul shall be joyful in my God; for he hath clothed me with the garments of salvation, he hath covered me with the robe of righteousness, as a bridegroom decketh *himself* with ornaments, and as a bride adorneth *herself* with her jewels.

Psalm 16:9

Therefore my heart is glad, and my glory rejoiceth: my flesh also shall rest in hope.

Psalm 16:11

Thou wilt shew me the path of life: in thy presence *is* fulness of joy; at thy right hand *there are* pleasures for evermore.

Jeremiah 15:16

Thy words were found, and I did eat them; and thy word was unto me the joy and rejoicing of mine heart: for I am called by thy name, O LORD God of hosts.

1 Peter 1:8

Whom having not seen, ye love; in whom, though now ye see *him* not, yet believing, ye rejoice with joy unspeakable and full of glory.

What pleases God?

Matthew 3:17
And lo a voice from heaven, saying, This is my beloved Son, in whom I am well pleased.

Hebrews 11:6
But without faith *it is* impossible to please *him:* for he that cometh to God must believe that he is, and *that* he is a rewarder of them that diligently seek him.

Hebrews 13:16
But to do good and to communicate forget not: for with such sacrifices God is well pleased.

Ephesians 1:5
Having predestinated us unto the adoption of children by Jesus Christ to himself, according to the good pleasure of his will.

Ephesians 1:9
Having made known unto us the mystery of his will, according to his good pleasure which he hath purposed in himself.

1 Thessalonians 2:4
But as we were allowed of God to be put in trust with the gospel, even so we speak; not as pleasing men, but God, which trieth our hearts.

1 Peter 2:20

For what glory *is it,* if, when ye be buffeted for your faults, ye shall take it patiently? but if, when ye do well, and suffer *for it,* ye take it patiently, this *is* acceptable with God.

PRAYER

How should I pray?

Ephesians 3:12
In whom we have boldness and access with confidence by the faith of him.

2 Chronicles 7:14
If my people, which are called by my name, shall humble themselves, and pray, and seek my face, and turn from their wicked ways; then will I hear from heaven, and will forgive their sin, and will heal their land.

Ephesians 6:18
Praying always with all prayer and supplication in the Spirit, and watching thereunto with all perseverance and supplication for all saints.

James 1:6
But let him ask in faith, nothing wavering. For he that wavereth is like a wave of the sea driven with the wind and tossed.

1 Peter 4:7
But the end of all things is at hand: be ye therefore sober, and watch unto prayer.

Ecclesiastes 5:2
Be not rash with thy mouth, and let not thine heart be

hasty to utter *any* thing before God: for God *is* in heaven, and thou upon earth: therefore let thy words be few.

Luke 18:1

And he spake a parable unto them *to this end,* that men ought always to pray, and not to faint.

Matthew 6:6

But thou, when thou prayest, enter into thy closet, and when thou hast shut thy door, pray to thy Father which is in secret; and thy Father which seeth in secret shall reward thee openly.

How did Jesus pray?

Matthew 14:23
And when he had sent the multitudes away, he went up into a mountain apart to pray: and when the evening was come, he was there alone.

Luke 5:16
And he withdrew himself into the wilderness, and prayed.

Mark 1:35
And in the morning, rising up a great while before day, he went out, and departed into a solitary place, and there prayed.

John 6:11
And Jesus took the loaves; and when he had given thanks, he distributed to the disciples, and the disciples to them that were set down; and likewise of the fishes as much as they would.

Luke 6:12
And it came to pass in those days, that he went out into a mountain to pray, and continued all night in prayer to God.

Hebrews 5:7

Who in the days of his flesh, when he had offered up prayers and supplications with strong crying and tears unto him that was able to save him from death, and was heard in that he feared.

Matthew 26:39

And he went a little farther, and fell on his face, and prayed, saying, O my Father, if it be possible, let this cup pass from me: nevertheless not as I will, but as thou *wilt.*

How do women and men of God pray?

1 Samuel 1:15
And Hannah answered and said, No, my lord, I *am* a woman of a sorrowful spirit: I have drunken neither wine nor strong drink, but have poured out my soul before the LORD.

1 Kings 8:22-23
And Solomon stood before the altar of the LORD in the presence of all the congregation of Israel, and spread forth his hands toward heaven: And he said, LORD God of Israel, *there is* no God like thee, in heaven above, or on earth beneath, who keepest covenant and mercy with thy servants that walk before thee with all their heart.

Nehemiah 2:4
Then the king said unto me, For what dost thou make request? So I prayed to the God of heaven.

Daniel 6:10
Now when Daniel knew that the writing was signed, he went into his house; and his windows being open in his chamber toward Jerusalem, he kneeled upon his knees three times a day, and prayed, and gave thanks before his God, as he did aforetime.

Luke 2:37

And she *was* a widow of about fourscore and four years, which departed not from the temple, but served *God* with fastings and prayers night and day.

Acts 10:9

On the morrow, as they went on their journey, and drew nigh unto the city, Peter went up upon the housetop to pray about the sixth hour.

Acts 12:5

Peter therefore was kept in prison: but prayer was made without ceasing of the church unto God for him.

Acts 16:25

And at midnight Paul and Silas prayed, and sang praises unto God: and the prisoners heard them.

What should I pray?

Psalm 38:18
For I will declare mine iniquity; I will be sorry for my sin.

1 Samuel 14:36
And Saul said, Let us go down after the Philistines by night, and spoil them until the morning light, and let us not leave a man of them. And they said, Do whatsoever seemeth good unto thee. Then said the priest, Let us draw near hither unto God.

Psalm 9:1-2
I will praise *thee,* O LORD, with my whole heart; I will shew forth all thy marvellous works. I will be glad and rejoice in thee: I will sing praise to thy name, O thou most High.

Psalm 50:15
And call upon me in the day of trouble: I will deliver thee, and thou shalt glorify me.

James 1:5
If any of you lack wisdom, let him ask of God, that giveth to all *men* liberally, and upbraideth not; and it shall be given him.

Matthew 9:37-38

Then saith he unto his disciples, The harvest truly *is* plenteous, but the labourers *are* few. Pray ye therefore the Lord of the harvest, that he will send forth laborers into his harvest.

Luke 11:2-3

And he said unto them, When ye pray, say, Our Father which art in heaven, Hallowed be thy name. Thy kingdom come. Thy will be done, as in heaven, so in earth. Give us day by day our daily bread.

Matthew 7:7-8

Ask, and it shall be given you; seek, and ye shall find; knock, and it shall be opened unto you: For every one that asketh receiveth; and he that seeketh findeth; and to him that knocketh it shall be opened.

For whom should I pray?

2 Thessalonians 1:11-12

Wherefore also we pray always for you, that our God would count you worthy of *this* calling, and fulfil all the good pleasure of *his* goodness, and the work of faith with power: That the name of our Lord Jesus Christ may be glorified in you, and ye in him, according to the grace of our God and the Lord Jesus Christ.

Ephesians 6:19

And for me, that utterance may be given unto me, that I may open my mouth boldly, to make known the mystery of the gospel.

1 Timothy 2:1-2

I exhort therefore, that, first of all, supplications, prayers, intercessions, *and* giving of thanks, be made for all men; For kings, and *for* all that are in authority; that we may lead a quiet and peaceable life in all godliness and honesty.

Job 1:5

And it was so, when the days of *their* feasting were gone about, that Job sent and sanctified them, and rose up early in the morning, and offered burnt offerings *according* to the number of them all: for Job said, It may be that my sons have sinned, and cursed God in their hearts. Thus did Job continually.

1 Samuel 12:23

Moreover as for me, God forbid that I should sin against the LORD in ceasing to pray for you: but I will teach you the good and the right way.

Matthew 5:44

But I say unto you, Love your enemies, bless them that curse you, do good to them that hate you, and pray for them which despitefully use you, and persecute you.

James 5:14-15

Is any sick among you? let him call for the elders of the church; and let them pray over him, anointing him with oil in the name of the Lord: And the prayer of faith shall save the sick, and the Lord shall raise him up; and if he have committed sins, they shall be forgiven him.

1 John 5:16

If any man see his brother sin a sin *which is* not unto death, he shall ask, and he shall give him life for them that sin not unto death. There is a sin unto death: I do not say that he shall pray for it.

Does God always hear my prayers?

Psalm 145:19

He will fulfil the desire of them that fear him: he also will hear their cry, and will save them.

1 Peter 3:12

For the eyes of the Lord *are* over the righteous, and his ears *are open* unto their prayers: but the face of the Lord *is* against them that do evil.

1 John 5:14

And this is the confidence that we have in him, that, if we ask any thing according to his will, he heareth us.

Psalm 145:18

The LORD *is* nigh unto all them that call upon him, to all that call upon him in truth.

Matthew 21:22

And all things, whatsoever ye shall ask in prayer, believing, ye shall receive.

James 5:16

Confess *your* faults one to another, and pray one for another, that ye may be healed. The effectual fervent prayer of a righteous man availeth much.

Isaiah 65:24

And it shall come to pass, that before they call, I will answer; and while they are yet speaking, I will hear.

2 Corinthians 12:8-9

For this thing I besought the Lord thrice, that it might depart from me. And he said unto me, My grace is sufficient for thee: for my strength is made perfect in weakness. Most gladly therefore will I rather glory in my infirmities, that the power of Christ may rest upon me.

REST

In whom do I find rest?

Psalm 4:8
I will both lay me down in peace, and sleep: for thou, Lord, only makest me dwell in safety.

Zephaniah 3:17
The Lord thy God in the midst of thee is mighty; he will save, he will rejoice over thee with joy; he will rest in his love, he will joy over thee with singing.

Psalm 62:5
My soul, wait thou only upon God; for my expectation is from him.

Psalm 23:1-2
The Lord is my shepherd; I shall not want. He maketh me to lie down in green pastures: he leadeth me beside the still waters.

2 Chronicles 14:11
And Asa cried unto the Lord his God, and said, Lord, it is nothing with thee to help, whether with many, or with them that have no power: help us, O Lord our God; for we rest on thee, and in thy name we go against this multitude. O Lord, thou art our God; let not man prevail against thee.

Psalm 16:9
Therefore my heart is glad, and my glory rejoiceth: my flesh also shall rest in hope.

Psalm 116:7
Return unto thy rest, O my soul; for the Lord hath dealt bountifully with thee.

How can I find rest?

Matthew 11:28-29
Come unto me, all ye that labour and are heavy laden, and I will give you rest. Take my yoke upon you, and learn of me; for I am meek and lowly in heart: and ye shall find rest unto your souls.

Psalm 46:10
Be still, and know that I am God: I will be exalted among the heathen, I will be exalted in the earth.

Psalm 37:7
Rest in the Lord, and wait patiently for him: fret not thyself because of him who prospereth in his way, because of the man who bringeth wicked devices to pass.

Psalm 107:28-30
Then they cry unto the Lord in their trouble, and he bringeth them out of their distresses. He maketh the storm a calm, so that the waves thereof are still. Then are they glad because they be quiet; so he bringeth them unto their desired haven.

2 Thessalonians 1:6-8
Seeing it is a righteous thing with God to recompense tribulation to them that trouble you; And to you who

are troubled rest with us, when the Lord Jesus shall be revealed from heaven with his mighty angels, In flaming fire taking vengeance on them that know not God, and that obey not the gospel of our Lord Jesus Christ.

How do I receive eternal rest?

Hebrews 4:3-10

For we which have believed do enter into rest, as he said, As I have sworn in my wrath, if they shall enter into my rest: although the works were finished from the foundation of the world. For he spake in a certain place of the seventh day on this wise, And God did rest the seventh day from all his works. And in this place again, If they shall enter into my rest. Seeing therefore it remaineth that some must enter therein, and they to whom it was first preached entered not in because of unbelief: Again, he limiteth a certain day, saying in David, To day, after so long a time; as it is said, To day if ye will hear his voice, harden not your hearts. For if Jesus had given them rest, then would he not afterward have spoken of another day. There remaineth therefore a rest to the people of God. For he that is entered into his rest, he also hath ceased from his own works, as God did from his.

Revelation 14:13

And I heard a voice from heaven saying unto me, Write, Blessed are the dead which die in the Lord from henceforth: Yea, saith the Spirit, that they may rest from their labours; and their works do follow them.

1 Chronicles 23:25

For David said, The Lord God of Israel hath given rest unto his people, that they may dwell in Jerusalem for ever.

RIGHTEOUSNESS

What is righteousness?

Deuteronomy 6:25
And it shall be our righteousness, if we observe to do all these commandments before the LORD our God, as he hath commanded us.

Romans 10:5
For Moses describeth the righteousness which is of the law, That the man which doeth those things shall live by them.

Luke 1:6
And they were both righteous before God, walking in all the commandments and ordinances of the Lord blameless.

Psalm 1:2
But his delight *is* in the law of the LORD; and in his law doth he meditate day and night.

Is anyone good enough for God?

Psalm 14:1
The fool hath said in his heart, *There is* no God. They are corrupt, they have done abominable works, *there is* none that doeth good.

Romans 7:18
For I know that in me (that is, in my flesh,) dwelleth no good thing: for to will is present with me; but *how* to perform that which is good I find not.

Proverbs 20:9
Who can say, I have made my heart clean, I am pure from my sin?

Isaiah 64:6
But we are all as an unclean *thing,* and all our righteousnesses *are* as filthy rags; and we all do fade as a leaf; and our iniquities, like the wind, have taken us away.

Romans 3:23
For all have sinned, and come short of the glory of God.

1 John 1:8
If we say that we have no sin, we deceive ourselves, and the truth is not in us.

How can I become righteous?

Genesis 15:6

And he believed in the LORD; and he counted it to him for righteousness.

Romans 10:4

For Christ *is* the end of the law for righteousness to every one that believeth.

Acts 13:39

And by him all that believe are justified from all things, from which ye could not be justified by the law of Moses.

Galatians 3:24

Wherefore the law was our schoolmaster *to bring us* unto Christ, that we might be justified by faith.

1 Corinthians 6:11

And such were some of you: but ye are washed, but ye are sanctified, but ye are justified in the name of the Lord Jesus, and by the Spirit of our God.

What results from righteousness?

Romans 4:7-8

Saying, Blessed *are* they whose iniquities are forgiven, and whose sins are covered. Blessed *is* the man to whom the Lord will not impute sin.

Matthew 5:6

Blessed *are* they which do hunger and thirst after righteousness: for they shall be filled.

1 Peter 3:14

But and if ye suffer for righteousness' sake, happy *are ye:* and be not afraid of their terror, neither be troubled.

Matthew 5:10

Blessed *are* they which are persecuted for righteousness' sake: for theirs is the kingdom of heaven.

Matthew 5:12

Rejoice, and be exceeding glad: for great *is* your reward in heaven: for so persecuted they the prophets which were before you.

Daniel 12:3

And they that be wise shall shine as the brightness of the firmament; and they that turn many to righteousness as the stars for ever and ever.

Isaiah 45:24-25

Surely, shall *one* say, in the LORD have I righteousness and strength: *even* to him shall *men* come; and all that are incensed against him shall be ashamed. In the LORD shall all the seed of Israel be justified, and shall glory.

SATISFACTION

What will truly satisfy me?

Psalm 107:8-9

Oh that *men* would praise the LORD *for* his goodness, and *for* his wonderful works to the children of men! For he satisfieth the longing soul, and filleth the hungry soul with goodness.

Psalm 90:14

O satisfy us early with thy mercy; that we may rejoice and be glad all our days.

Psalm 119:35

Make me to go in the path of thy commandments; for therein do I delight.

John 6:35

And Jesus said unto them, I am the bread of life: he that cometh to me shall never hunger; and he that believeth on me shall never thirst.

John 4:13

Jesus answered and said unto her, Whosoever drinketh of this water shall thirst again.

John 4:14

But whosoever drinketh of the water that I shall give him shall never thirst; but the water that I shall give him shall be in him a well of water springing up into everlasting life.

1 Timothy 6:6
But godliness with contentment is great gain.

How can I find satisfaction in the midst of hardship?

2 Corinthians 12:10

Therefore I take pleasure in infirmities, in reproaches, in necessities, in persecutions, in distresses for Christ's sake: for when I am weak, then am I strong.

Job 1:21

And said, Naked came I out of my mother's womb, and naked shall I return thither: the LORD gave, and the LORD hath taken away; blessed be the name of the LORD.

Psalm 37:4

Delight thyself also in the LORD; and he shall give thee the desires of thine heart.

Psalm 63:5

My soul shall be satisfied as *with* marrow and fatness; and my mouth shall praise *thee* with joyful lips.

Psalm 63:6

When I remember thee upon my bed, *and* meditate on thee in the *night* watches.

Matthew 5:6

Blessed *are* they which do hunger and thirst after righteousness: for they shall be filled.

Philippians 4:11-13

Not that I speak in respect of want: for I have learned, in whatsoever state I am, *therewith* to be content. I know both how to be abased, and I know how to abound: every where and in all things I am instructed both to be full and to be hungry, both to abound and to suffer need. I can do all things through Christ which strengtheneth me.

What will not satisfy me?

Hebrews 13:5

Let your conversation *be* without covetousness; *and be* content with such things as ye have: for he hath said, I will never leave thee, nor forsake thee.

1 Timothy 6:17

Charge them that are rich in this world, that they be not highminded, nor trust in uncertain riches, but in the living God, who giveth us richly all things to enjoy.

Ecclesiastes 5:10

He that loveth silver shall not be satisfied with silver; nor he that loveth abundance with increase: this *is* also vanity.

1 Timothy 6:6-7

But godliness with contentment is great gain. For we brought nothing into *this* world, *and it is* certain we can carry nothing out.

Isaiah 55:2

Wherefore do ye spend money for *that which is* not bread? and your labour for *that which* satisfieth not? hearken diligently unto me, and eat ye *that which is* good, and let your soul delight itself in fatness.

Ecclesiastes 2:10-11

And whatsoever mine eyes desired I kept not from them, I withheld not my heart from any joy; for my heart rejoiced in all my labour: and this was my portion of all my labour. Then I looked on all the works that my hands had wrought, and on the labour that I had laboured to do: and, behold, all *was* vanity and vexation of spirit, and *there was* no profit under the sun.

SELF-CONTROL

Does God want me to be self-controlled?

2 Timothy 1:7
For God hath not given us the spirit of fear; but of power, and of love, and of a sound mind.

1 Peter 4:7
But the end of all things is at hand: be ye therefore sober, and watch unto prayer.

Psalm 4:4
Stand in awe, and sin not: commune with your own heart upon your bed, and be still.

1 Peter 5:8
Be sober, be vigilant; because your adversary the devil, as a roaring lion, walketh about, seeking whom he may devour.

Proverbs 25:28
He that *hath* no rule over his own spirit *is like* a city *that is* broken down, *and* without walls.

Can self-control help me to conquer sin?

1 Thessalonians 5:6-8

Therefore let us not sleep, as *do* others; but let us watch and be sober. For they that sleep sleep in the night; and they that be drunken are drunken in the night. But let us, who are of the day, be sober, putting on the breastplate of faith and love; and for an helmet, the hope of salvation.

Titus 2:11-12

For the grace of God that bringeth salvation hath appeared to all men, Teaching us that, denying ungodliness and worldly lusts, we should live soberly, righteously, and godly, in this present world.

1 Peter 1:13-15

Wherefore gird up the loins of your mind, be sober, and hope to the end for the grace that is to be brought unto you at the revelation of Jesus Christ; As obedient children, not fashioning yourselves according to the former lusts in your ignorance: But as he which hath called you is holy, so be ye holy in all manner of conversation.

Is self-control a mark of God's leaders?

1 Timothy 3:2

A bishop then must be blameless, the husband of one wife, vigilant, sober, of good behaviour, given to hospitality, apt to teach.

Titus 1:7-8

For a bishop must be blameless, as the steward of God; not selfwilled, not soon angry, not given to wine, no striker, not given to filthy lucre; But a lover of hospitality, a lover of good men, sober, just, holy, temperate.

Titus 2:2-6

That the aged men be sober, grave, temperate, sound in faith, in charity, in patience. The aged women likewise, that *they be* in behaviour as becometh holiness, not false accusers, not given to much wine, teachers of good things; That they may teach the young women to be sober, to love their husbands, to love their children, *To be* discreet, chaste, keepers at home, good, obedient to their own husbands, that the word of God be not blasphemed. Young men likewise exhort to be sober minded.

SPEECH

Should I be careful of what I say?

James 1:26

If any man among you seem to be religious, and bridleth not his tongue, but deceiveth his own heart, this man's religion *is* vain.

James 3:8-10

But the tongue can no man tame; *it is* an unruly evil, full of deadly poison. Therewith bless we God, even the Father; and therewith curse we men, which are made after the similitude of God. Out of the same mouth proceedeth blessing and cursing. My brethren, these things ought not so to be.

Proverbs 13:2-3

A man shall eat good by the fruit of *his* mouth: but the soul of the transgressors *shall eat* violence. He that keepeth his mouth keepeth his life: *but* he that openeth wide his lips shall have destruction.

Matthew 12:34

O generation of vipers, how can ye, being evil, speak good things? for out of the abundance of the heart the mouth speaketh.

Matthew 12:36-37

But I say unto you, That every idle word that men shall

speak, they shall give account thereof in the day of judgment. For by thy words thou shalt be justified, and by thy words thou shalt be condemned.

James 3:5-6

Even so the tongue is a little member, and boasteth great things. Behold, how great a matter a little fire kindleth! And the tongue *is* a fire, a world of iniquity: so is the tongue among our members, that it defileth the whole body, and setteth on fire the course of nature; and it is set on fire of hell.

How does speech relate powerfully to my faith?

Romans 10:8-10

But what saith it? The word is nigh thee, *even* in thy mouth, and in thy heart: that is, the word of faith, which we preach; That if thou shalt confess with thy mouth the Lord Jesus, and shalt believe in thine heart that God hath raised him from the dead, thou shalt be saved. For with the heart man believeth unto righteousness; and with the mouth confession is made unto salvation.

Mark 11:23

For verily I say unto you, That whosoever shall say unto this mountain, Be thou removed, and be thou cast into the sea; and shall not doubt in his heart, but shall believe that those things which he saith shall come to pass; he shall have whatsoever he saith.

Luke 17:6

And the Lord said, If ye had faith as a grain of mustard seed, ye might say unto this sycamine tree, Be thou plucked up by the root, and be thou planted in the sea; and it should obey you.

2 Corinthians 4:13-14

We having the same spirit of faith, according as it is

written, I believed, and therefore have I spoken; we also believe, and therefore speak; Knowing that he which raised up the Lord Jesus shall raise up us also by Jesus, and shall present *us* with you.

Should my words carry wisdom?

Proverbs 12:18
There is that speaketh like the piercings of a sword: but the tongue of the wise *is* health.

Proverbs 12:22
Lying lips *are* abomination to the LORD: but they that deal truly *are* his delight.

Proverbs 16:13
Righteous lips *are* the delight of kings; and they love him that speaketh right.

Proverbs 16:21
The wise in heart shall be called prudent: and the sweetness of the lips increaseth learning.

Proverbs 16:23-24
The heart of the wise teacheth his mouth, and addeth learning to his lips. Pleasant words *are as* an honeycomb, sweet to the soul, and health to the bones.

Proverbs 16:27-28
An ungodly man diggeth up evil: and in his lips *there is* as a burning fire. A froward man soweth strife: and a whisperer separateth chief friends.

Proverbs 18:4
The words of a man's mouth *are as* deep waters, *and* the wellspring of wisdom *as* a flowing brook.

Proverbs 18:7
A fool's mouth *is* his destruction, and his lips *are* the snare of his soul.

Proverbs 18:20-21
A man's belly shall be satisfied with the fruit of his mouth; *and* with the increase of his lips shall he be filled. Death and life *are* in the power of the tongue: and they that love it shall eat the fruit thereof.

James 3:13
Who *is* a wise man and endued with knowledge among you? let him shew out of a good conversation his works with meekness of wisdom.

STRENGTH

Who is my source of strength?

Psalm 46:10

Be still, and know that I *am* God: I will be exalted among the heathen, I will be exalted in the earth.

Proverbs 18:10

The name of the LORD *is* a strong tower: the righteous runneth into it, and is safe.

Psalm 84:5

Blessed *is* the man whose strength *is* in thee; in whose heart *are* the ways *of them*.

Isaiah 40:31

But they that wait upon the LORD shall renew *their* strength; they shall mount up with wings as eagles; they shall run, and not be weary; *and* they shall walk, and not faint.

Isaiah 33:2

O LORD, be gracious unto us; we have waited for thee: be thou their arm every morning, our salvation also in the time of trouble.

Nehemiah 8:10

Then he said unto them, Go your way, eat the fat, and drink the sweet, and send portions unto them for whom nothing is prepared: for *this* day *is* holy unto our Lord: neither be ye sorry; for the joy of the LORD is your strength.

Will God arm me with strength?

Isaiah 41:10

Fear thou not; for I *am* with thee: be not dismayed; for I *am* thy God: I will strengthen thee; yea, I will help thee; yea, I will uphold thee with the right hand of my righteousness.

Philippians 4:13

I can do all things through Christ which strengtheneth me.

Psalm 73:26

My flesh and my heart faileth: *but* God *is* the strength of my heart, and my portion for ever.

2 Samuel 22:33-34

God *is* my strength *and* power: and he maketh my way perfect. He maketh my feet like hinds' *feet:* and setteth me upon my high places.

Psalm 29:11

The LORD will give strength unto his people; the LORD will bless his people with peace.

Exodus 15:2

The LORD *is* my strength and song, and he is become my salvation: he *is* my God, and I will prepare him an habitation; my father's God, and I will exalt him.

Psalm 59:16
But I will sing of thy power; yea, I will sing aloud of thy mercy in the morning: for thou hast been my defence and refuge in the day of my trouble.

Does God's strength fulfill my weakness?

2 Corinthians 12:9

And he said unto me, My grace is sufficient for thee: for my strength is made perfect in weakness. Most gladly therefore will I rather glory in my infirmities, that the power of Christ may rest upon me.

Isaiah 40:29

He giveth power to the faint; and to *them that have* no might he increaseth strength.

Ezekiel 34:16

I will seek that which was lost, and bring again that which was driven away, and will bind up *that which was* broken, and will strengthen that which was sick: but I will destroy the fat and the strong; I will feed them with judgment.

SUFFERING

What causes suffering?

Romans 8:17
And if children, then heirs; heirs of God, and joint-heirs with Christ; if so be that we suffer with *him,* that we may be also glorified together.

2 Timothy 3:12
Yea, and all that will live godly in Christ Jesus shall suffer persecution.

Hebrews 11:25
Choosing rather to suffer affliction with the people of God, than to enjoy the pleasures of sin for a season.

Leviticus 26:43
The land also shall be left of them, and shall enjoy her sabbaths, while she lieth desolate without them: and they shall accept of the punishment of their iniquity: because, even because they despised my judgments, and because their soul abhorred my statutes.

Jeremiah 32:18
Thou shewest lovingkindness unto thousands, and recompensest the iniquity of the fathers into the bosom of their children after them: the Great, the Mighty God, the LORD of hosts, *is* his name.

John 9:1-3

And as *Jesus* passed by, he saw a man which was blind from *his* birth. And his disciples asked him, saying, Master, who did sin, this man, or his parents, that he was born blind? Jesus answered, Neither hath this man sinned, nor his parents: but that the works of God should be made manifest in him.

Why does God allow me to suffer?

1 Peter 4:12

Beloved, think it not strange concerning the fiery trial which is to try you, as though some strange thing happened unto you.

Isaiah 55:8-9

For my thoughts *are* not your thoughts, neither *are* your ways my ways, saith the LORD. For *as* the heavens are higher than the earth, so are my ways higher than your ways, and my thoughts than your thoughts.

Romans 8:28

And we know that all things work together for good to them that love God, to them who are the called according to *his* purpose.

2 Corinthians 4:11

For we which live are alway delivered unto death for Jesus' sake, that the life also of Jesus might be made manifest in our mortal flesh.

Deuteronomy 8:2

And thou shalt remember all the way which the LORD thy God led thee these forty years in the wilderness, to humble thee, *and* to prove thee, to know what *was* in thine heart, whether thou wouldest keep his commandments, or no.

Proverbs 3:11-12

My son, despise not the chastening of the LORD; neither be weary of his correction: For whom the LORD loveth he correcteth; even as a father the son *in whom* he delighteth.

Can suffering produce good?

2 Timothy 2:10

Therefore I endure all things for the elect's sakes, that they may also obtain the salvation which is in Christ Jesus with eternal glory.

1 Peter 4:14

If ye be reproached for the name of Christ, happy *are ye;* for the spirit of glory and of God resteth upon you: on their part he is evil spoken of, but on your part he is glorified.

2 Corinthians 1:5

For as the sufferings of Christ abound in us, so our consolation also aboundeth by Christ.

Romans 4:3-5

For what saith the scripture? Abraham believed God, and it was counted unto him for righteousness. Now to him that worketh is the reward not reckoned of grace, but of debt. But to him that worketh not, but believeth on him that justifieth the ungodly, his faith is counted for righteousness.

James 1:3

Knowing *this,* that the trying of your faith worketh patience.

Hebrews 12:11

Now no chastening for the present seemeth to be joyous, but grievous: nevertheless afterward it yieldeth the peaceable fruit of righteousness unto them which are exercised thereby.

Psalm 126:5-6

They that sow in tears shall reap in joy. He that goeth forth and weepeth, bearing precious seed, shall doubtless come again with rejoicing, bringing his sheaves *with him.*

What comfort can I have in the midst of suffering?

Psalm 18:30

As for God, his way *is* perfect: the word of the LORD is tried: he *is* a buckler to all those that trust in him.

Romans 8:35-37

Who shall separate us from the love of Christ? *shall* tribulation, or distress, or persecution, or famine, or nakedness, or peril, or sword? As it is written, For thy sake we are killed all the day long; we are accounted as sheep for the slaughter. Nay, in all these things we are more than conquerors through him that loved us.

Lamentations 3:32-33

But though he cause grief, yet will he have compassion according to the multitude of his mercies. For he doth not afflict willingly nor grieve the children of men.

Psalm 22:24

For he hath not despised nor abhorred the affliction of the afflicted; neither hath he hid his face from him; but when he cried unto him, he heard.

Luke 24:26

Ought not Christ to have suffered these things, and to enter into his glory?

Hebrews 2:18
For in that he himself hath suffered being tempted, he is able to succour them that are tempted.

Romans 8:18
For I reckon that the sufferings of this present time *are* not worthy *to be compared* with the glory which shall be revealed in us.

How can I endure suffering?

Psalm 55:22

Cast thy burden upon the LORD, and he shall sustain thee: he shall never suffer the righteous to be moved.

Isaiah 41:10

Fear thou not; for I *am* with thee: be not dismayed; for I *am* thy God: I will strengthen thee; yea, I will help thee; yea, I will uphold thee with the right hand of my righteousness.

Hebrews 10:23

Let us hold fast the profession of *our* faith without wavering (for he is faithful that promised).

1 Peter 2:20

For what glory *is it,* if, when ye be buffeted for your faults, ye shall take it patiently? but if, when ye do well, and suffer *for it,* ye take it patiently, this *is* acceptable with God.

2 Corinthians 12:10

Therefore I take pleasure in infirmities, in reproaches, in necessities, in persecutions, in distresses for Christ's sake: for when I am weak, then am I strong.

1 Peter 4:13

But rejoice, inasmuch as ye are partakers of Christ's sufferings; that, when his glory shall be revealed, ye may be glad also with exceeding joy.

Philippians 1:29

For unto you it is given in the behalf of Christ, not only to believe on him, but also to suffer for his sake.

2 Corinthians 1:3-4

Blessed *be* God, even the Father of our Lord Jesus Christ, the Father of mercies, and the God of all comfort; Who comforteth us in all our tribulation, that we may be able to comfort them which are in any trouble, by the comfort wherewith we ourselves are comforted of God.

1 Peter 4:13

[illegible]

[illegible]

Philippians 3:20

[illegible]

[illegible]

2 Corinthians 12:8

[illegible] Jesus, the author [illegible] and the [illegible]

[illegible]

[illegible]

[illegible]

TRUST

What shouldn't I trust in?

Psalm 118:8-9

It is better to trust in the Lord than to put confidence in man. It is better to trust in the Lord than to put confidence in princes.

Proverbs 29:25

The fear of man bringeth a snare: but whoso putteth his trust in the Lord shall be safe.

Job 15:31

Let not him that is deceived trust in vanity: for vanity shall be his recompence.

Psalm 31:6

I have hated them that regard lying vanities: but I trust in the Lord.

Psalm 44:6-8

For I will not trust in my bow, neither shall my sword save me. But thou hast saved us from our enemies, and hast put them to shame that hated us. In God we boast all the day long, and praise thy name for ever.

Proverbs 3:5-6

Trust in the Lord with all thine heart; and lean not unto thine own understanding. In all thy ways acknowledge him, and he shall direct thy paths.

Psalm 62:10

Trust not in oppression, and become not vain in robbery: if riches increase, set not your heart upon them.

Philippians 3:4-11

Though I might also have confidence in the flesh. If any other man thinketh that he hath whereof he might trust in the flesh, I more: Circumcised the eighth day, of the stock of Israel, of the tribe of Benjamin, an Hebrew of the Hebrews; as touching the law, a Pharisee; Concerning zeal, persecuting the church; touching the righteousness which is in the law, blameless. But what things were gain to me, those I counted loss for Christ. Yea doubtless, and I count all things but loss for the excellency of the knowledge of Christ Jesus my Lord: for whom I have suffered the loss of all things, and do count them but dung, that I may win Christ, And be found in him, not having mine own righteousness, which is of the law, but that which is through the faith of Christ, the righteousness which is of God by faith: That I may know him, and the power of his resurrection, and the fellowship of his sufferings, being made conformable unto his death; If by any means I might attain unto the resurrection of the dead.

Can I trust in money?

1 Timothy 6:17
Charge them that are rich in this world, that they be not highminded, nor trust in uncertain riches, but in the living God, who giveth us richly all things to enjoy.

Psalm 49:6-7
They that trust in their wealth, and boast themselves in the multitude of their riches; None of them can by any means redeem his brother, nor give to God a ransom for him.

Mark 10:24
And the disciples were astonished at his words. But Jesus answereth again, and saith unto them, Children, how hard is it for them that trust in riches to enter into the kingdom of God!

Can I trust God to deal with my enemies?

Psalm 18:2-3

The Lord is my rock, and my fortress, and my deliverer; my God, my strength, in whom I will trust; my buckler, and the horn of my salvation, and my high tower. I will call upon the Lord, who is worthy to be praised: so shall I be saved from mine enemies.

Psalm 11:1-7

In the Lord put I my trust: How say ye to my soul, Flee as a bird to your mountain? For, lo, the wicked bend their bow, they make ready their arrow upon the string, that they may privily shoot at the upright in heart. If the foundations be destroyed, what can the righteous do? The Lord is in his holy temple, the Lord's throne is in heaven: his eyes behold, his eyelids try, the children of men. The Lord trieth the righteous: but the wicked and him that loveth violence his soul hateth. Upon the wicked he shall rain snares, fire and brimstone, and an horrible tempest: this shall be the portion of their cup. For the righteous Lord loveth righteousness; his countenance doth behold the upright.

Psalm 25:1-3

Unto thee, O Lord, do I lift up my soul. O my God, I trust in thee: let me not be ashamed, let not mine enemies triumph over me. Yea, let none that wait on thee be ashamed: let them be ashamed which transgress without cause.

Psalm 7:1-2

O Lord my God, in thee do I put my trust: save me from all them that persecute me, and deliver me: Lest he tear my soul like a lion, rending it in pieces, while there is none to deliver.

Psalm 55:23

But thou, O God, shalt bring them down into the pit of destruction: bloody and deceitful men shall not live out half their days; but I will trust in thee.

In whom should I place my trust?

Psalm 20:7
Some trust in chariots, and some in horses: but we will remember the name of the Lord our God.

2 Corinthians 1:9-10
But we had the sentence of death in ourselves, that we should not trust in ourselves, but in God which raiseth the dead: Who delivered us from so great a death, and doth deliver: in whom we trust that he will yet deliver us.

Psalm 4:5
Offer the sacrifices of righteousness, and put your trust in the Lord.

Psalm 64:10
The righteous shall be glad in the Lord, and shall trust in him; and all the upright in heart shall glory.

2 Samuel 22:2-3
And he said, The Lord is my rock, and my fortress, and my deliverer; The God of my rock; in him will I trust: he is my shield, and the horn of my salvation, my high tower, and my refuge, my saviour; thou savest me from violence.

Psalm 40:3-4

And he hath put a new song in my mouth, even praise unto our God: many shall see it, and fear, and shall trust in the Lord. Blessed is that man that maketh the Lord his trust, and respecteth not the proud, nor such as turn aside to lies.

Psalm 119:42

So shall I have wherewith to answer him that reproacheth me: for I trust in thy word.

1 Timothy 4:10

For therefore we both labour and suffer reproach, because we trust in the living God, who is the Saviour of all men, specially of those that believe.

Why should I trust in God?

Psalm 31:19

Oh how great is thy goodness, which thou hast laid up for them that fear thee; which thou hast wrought for them that trust in thee before the sons of men!

Psalm 37:3-6

Trust in the Lord, and do good; so shalt thou dwell in the land, and verily thou shalt be fed. Delight thyself also in the Lord; and he shall give thee the desires of thine heart. Commit thy way unto the Lord; trust also in him; and he shall bring it to pass. And he shall bring forth thy righteousness as the light, and thy judgment as the noonday.

Psalm 34:22

The Lord redeemeth the soul of his servants: and none of them that trust in him shall be desolate.

Isaiah 12:2

Behold, God is my salvation; I will trust, and not be afraid: for the Lord Jehovah is my strength and my song; he also is become my salvation.

Psalm 17:6-7

I have called upon thee, for thou wilt hear me, O God: incline thine ear unto me, and hear my speech. Shew thy marvellous lovingkindness, O thou that savest by thy right hand them which put their trust in thee from those that rise up against them.

Psalm 2:11-12
Serve the Lord with fear, and rejoice with trembling. Kiss the Son, lest he be angry, and ye perish from the way, when his wrath is kindled but a little. Blessed are all they that put their trust in him.

2 Samuel 22:31-32
As for God, his way is perfect; the word of the Lord is tried: he is a buckler to all them that trust in him. For who is God, save the Lord? and who is a rock, save our God?

Psalm 5:11-12
But let all those that put their trust in thee rejoice: let them ever shout for joy, because thou defendest them: let them also that love thy name be joyful in thee. For thou, Lord, wilt bless the righteous; with favour wilt thou compass him as with a shield.

Psalm 73:28
But it is good for me to draw near to God: I have put my trust in the Lord God, that I may declare all thy works.

When should I trust in God?

Psalm 62:8
Trust in him at all times; ye people, pour out your heart before him: God is a refuge for us.

Psalm 56:3
What time I am afraid, I will trust in thee.

Nahum 1:7
The Lord is good, a strong hold in the day of trouble; and he knoweth them that trust in him.

Psalm 143:8
Cause me to hear thy lovingkindness in the morning; for in thee do I trust: cause me to know the way wherein I should walk; for I lift up my soul unto thee.

TRUTH

What is truth?

Deuteronomy 32:4

He is the Rock, his work *is* perfect: for all his ways *are* judgment: a God of truth and without iniquity, just and right *is* he.

John 1:17

For the law was given by Moses, *but* grace and truth came by Jesus Christ.

John 17:17

Sanctify them through thy truth: thy word is truth.

Ephesians 6:14

Stand therefore, having your loins girt about with truth, and having on the breastplate of righteousness.

1 Peter 1:22

Seeing ye have purified your souls in obeying the truth through the Spirit unto unfeigned love of the brethren, *see that ye* love one another with a pure heart fervently.

John 17:19

And for their sakes I sanctify myself, that they also might be sanctified through the truth.

How can I be truthful?

Zechariah 8:16
These *are* the things that ye shall do; Speak ye every man the truth to his neighbour; execute the judgment of truth and peace in your gates.

Ephesians 4:25
Wherefore putting away lying, speak every man truth with his neighbour: for we are members one of another.

Proverbs 16:11
A just weight and balance *are* the LORD's: all the weights of the bag *are* his work.

Joshua 24:14
Now therefore fear the LORD, and serve him in sincerity and in truth: and put away the gods which your fathers served on the other side of the flood, and in Egypt; and serve ye the LORD.

Malachi 2:6
The law of truth was in his mouth, and iniquity was not found in his lips: he walked with me in peace and equity, and did turn many away from iniquity.

1 Peter 2:22
Who did no sin, neither was guile found in his mouth.

Ephesians 5:9
For the fruit of the Spirit is in all goodness and righteousness and truth.

What is deception?

Proverbs 24:28
Be not a witness against thy neighbour without cause; and deceive *not* with thy lips.

Psalm 119:118
Thou hast trodden down all them that err from thy statutes: for their deceit *is* falsehood.

Proverbs 26:28
A lying tongue hateth *those that are* afflicted by it; and a flattering mouth worketh ruin.

Proverbs 27:6
Faithful *are* the wounds of a friend; but the kisses of an enemy *are* deceitful.

Jeremiah 9:8
Their tongue *is as* an arrow shot out; it speaketh deceit: *one* speaketh peaceably to his neighbour with his mouth, but in heart he layeth his wait.

Proverbs 26:24
He that hateth dissembleth with his lips, and layeth up deceit within him.

How does God reward those who are truthful?

Proverbs 20:28
Mercy and truth preserve the king: and his throne is upholden by mercy.

Proverbs 12:19
The lip of truth shall be established for ever: but a lying tongue *is* but for a moment.

Deuteronomy 25:13-15
Thou shalt not have in thy bag divers weights, a great and a small. Thou shalt not have in thine house divers measures, a great and a small. *But* thou shalt have a perfect and just weight, a perfect and just measure shalt thou have: that thy days may be lengthened in the land which the LORD thy God giveth thee.

Psalm 32:2
Blessed *is* the man unto whom the LORD imputeth not iniquity, and in whose spirit *there is* no guile.

Psalm 37:37
Mark the perfect *man,* and behold the upright: for the end of *that* man *is* peace.

Psalm 24:3-4

Who shall ascend into the hill of the LORD? or who shall stand in his holy place? He that hath clean hands, and a pure heart; who hath not lifted up his soul unto vanity, nor sworn deceitfully.

How does God punish liars?

Luke 16:10

He that is faithful in that which is least is faithful also in much: and he that is unjust in the least is unjust also in much.

Isaiah 59:2-3

But your iniquities have separated between you and your God, and your sins have hid *his* face from you, that he will not hear. For your hands are defiled with blood, and your fingers with iniquity; your lips have spoken lies, your tongue hath muttered perverseness.

Revelation 21:27

And there shall in no wise enter into it any thing that defileth, neither *whatsoever* worketh abomination, or *maketh* a lie: but they which are written in the Lamb's book of life.

Proverbs 26:26

Whose hatred is covered by deceit, his wickedness shall be shewed before the *whole* congregation.

Psalm 55:23

But thou, O God, shalt bring them down into the pit of destruction: bloody and deceitful men shall not live out half their days; but I will trust in thee.

Revelation 21:8

But the fearful, and unbelieving, and the abominable, and murderers, and whoremongers, and sorcerers, and idolaters, and all liars, shall have their part in the lake which burneth with fire and brimstone: which is the second death.

Can lying ever be good?

1 John 2:21
I have not written unto you because ye know not the truth, but because ye know it, and that no lie is of the truth.

Romans 3:13
Their throat *is* an open sepulchre; with their tongues they have used deceit; the poison of asps *is* under their lips.

Colossians 3:9
Lie not one to another, seeing that ye have put off the old man with his deeds.

Proverbs 6:16, 19
These six *things* doth the LORD hate: yea, seven *are* an abomination unto him...A false witness *that* speaketh lies, and he that soweth discord among brethren.

John 8:44
Ye are of your father the devil, and the lusts of *your* father ye will do. He was a murderer from the beginning, and abode not in the truth, because there is no truth in him. When he speaketh a lie, he speaketh of his own: for he is a liar, and the father of it.

Hebrews 6:18
That by two immutable things, in which *it was* impossible for God to lie, we might have a strong consolation, who have fled for refuge to lay hold upon the hope set before us.

Should I ever lie?

Leviticus 19:11
Ye shall not steal, neither deal falsely, neither lie one to another.

Proverbs 12:22
Lying lips *are* abomination to the LORD: but they that deal truly *are* his delight.

Psalm 5:6
Thou shalt destroy them that speak leasing: the LORD will abhor the bloody and deceitful man.

Psalm 101:7
He that worketh deceit shall not dwell within my house: he that telleth lies shall not tarry in my sight.

Proverbs 19:5
A false witness shall not be unpunished, and *he that* speaketh lies shall not escape.

Proverbs 21:6
The getting of treasures by a lying tongue *is* a vanity tossed to and fro of them that seek death.

WISDOM

Is God the giver of all wisdom?

James 1:5

If any of you lack wisdom, let him ask of God, that giveth to all *men* liberally, and upbraideth not; and it shall be given him.

1 Corinthians 1:25

Because the foolishness of God is wiser than men; and the weakness of God is stronger than men.

Psalm 111:10

The fear of the LORD *is* the beginning of wisdom: a good understanding have all they that do *his commandments:* his praise endureth for ever.

James 3:17

But the wisdom that is from above is first pure, then peaceable, gentle, *and* easy to be intreated, full of mercy and good fruits, without partiality, and without hypocrisy.

Should I desire and seek wisdom?

Proverbs 4:7

Wisdom *is* the principal thing; *therefore* get wisdom: and with all thy getting get understanding.

Proverbs 24:14

So *shall* the knowledge of wisdom *be* unto thy soul: when thou hast found *it,* then there shall be a reward, and thy expectation shall not be cut off.

Ecclesiastes 7:11-12

Wisdom *is* good with an inheritance: and *by it there is* profit to them that see the sun. For wisdom *is* a defence, *and* money *is* a defence: but the excellency of knowledge *is, that* wisdom giveth life to them that have it.

Proverbs 16:16

How much better *is it* to get wisdom than gold! and to get understanding rather to be chosen than silver!

Ecclesiastes 8:1

Who *is* as the wise *man?* and who knoweth the interpretation of a thing? a man's wisdom maketh his face to shine, and the boldness of his face shall be changed.

WORSHIP

Why does God deserve my worship?

1 Chronicles 16:25

For great *is* the LORD, and greatly to be praised: he also *is* to be feared above all gods.

Psalm 29:2

Give unto the LORD the glory due unto his name; worship the LORD in the beauty of holiness.

Psalm 95:6

O come, let us worship and bow down: let us kneel before the LORD our maker.

Exodus 34:14

For thou shalt worship no other god: for the LORD, whose name *is* Jealous, *is* a jealous God.

Exodus 15:1-2

Then sang Moses and the children of Israel this song unto the LORD, and spake, saying, I will sing unto the LORD, for he hath triumphed gloriously: the horse and his rider hath he thrown into the sea. The LORD *is* my strength and song, and he is become my salvation: he *is* my God, and I will prepare him an habitation; my father's God, and I will exalt him.

How should I worship?

Hebrews 12:28

Wherefore we receiving a kingdom which cannot be moved, let us have grace, whereby we may serve God acceptably with reverence and godly fear.

Romans 12:1

I beseech you therefore, brethren, by the mercies of God, that ye present your bodies a living sacrifice, holy, acceptable unto God, *which is* your reasonable service.

John 4:23-24

But the hour cometh, and now is, when the true worshippers shall worship the Father in spirit and in truth: for the Father seeketh such to worship him. God *is* a Spirit: and they that worship him must worship *him* in spirit and in truth.

Psalm 100:2

Serve the LORD with gladness: come before his presence with singing.

Psalm 43:4

Then will I go unto the altar of God, unto God my exceeding joy: yea, upon the harp will I praise thee, O God my God.

What words of praise can I learn from the Bible?

Psalm 9:1-2
I will praise *thee,* O LORD, with my whole heart; I will shew forth all thy marvellous works. I will be glad and rejoice in thee: I will sing praise to thy name, O thou most High.

Psalm 139:14
I will praise thee; for I am fearfully *and* wonderfully made: marvellous *are* thy works; and *that* my soul knoweth right well.

Ephesians 1:3
Blessed *be* the God and Father of our Lord Jesus Christ, who hath blessed us with all spiritual blessings in heavenly *places* in Christ.

Psalm 52:9
I will praise thee for ever, because thou hast done *it:* and I will wait on thy name; for *it is* good before thy saints.

Psalm 28:6
Blessed *be* the LORD, because he hath heard the voice of my supplications.

2 Samuel 22:47

The LORD liveth; and blessed *be* my rock; and exalted be the God of the rock of my salvation.

Psalm 103:2-4

Bless the LORD, O my soul, and forget not all his benefits: Who forgiveth all thine iniquities; who healeth all thy diseases; Who redeemeth thy life from destruction; who crowneth thee with lovingkindness and tender mercies.

1 Peter 1:3

Blessed *be* the God and Father of our Lord Jesus Christ, which according to his abundant mercy hath begotten us again unto a lively hope by the resurrection of Jesus Christ from the dead.

2 Samuel 22:47

The LORD liveth; and blessed *be* my rock; and exalted be the God of the rock of my salvation.

Psalm 103:2-4

Bless the LORD, O my soul, and forget not all his benefits: Who forgiveth all thine iniquities; who healeth all thy diseases; Who redeemeth thy life from destruction; who crowneth thee with lovingkindness and tender mercies.

1 Peter 1:3

Blessed *be* the God and Father of our Lord Jesus Christ, which according to his abundant mercy hath begotten us again unto a lively hope by the resurrection of Jesus Christ from the dead.